D0916965

Landscapes

Landscapes

Selected Writings of J. B. Jackson

Edited by Ervin H. Zube

The University of Massachusetts Press 1970

Set in Monotype Ehrhardt and
printed in the United States of America
Designed by Richard Hendel

Foreword

J. B. Jackson is a highly articulate interpreter and critic of
the American landscape. He views the landscape with the
perspective of history, as a reflection of social values and
cultural patterns—as the expression of a way of life—as a
social and political landscape.

His focus is on the landscape that man is a part of, not
apart from—the humanized landscape. It transcends the
presently popular interest in the man-land relationship,
which most often implies a biological relationship to encom-
pass social and aesthetic-sensory concerns, "man's relation
to the world and to his fellow man."

From 1951 to 1968, readers of *Landscape*, a journal which he
founded and edited, were the fortunate audience for his per-
ceptive and penetrating essays and notes on the humanized
landscape. This book includes a collection of his writings
from *Landscape* and several lectures which were presented
at the University of Massachusetts in 1965 and 1966. I am
deeply grateful to both Mr. J. B. Jackson and the present
editor of *Landscape*, Mr. Blair Boyd, for their permission to
use the materials included in this book.

Ervin H. Zube

Contents

Jefferson, Thoreau & After

IN THE LONG chronicle of our American distrust of the city, two names stand out above the rest: Jefferson and Thoreau. One sought to destroy the city by political means; the other, fleeing it for the wilderness, wrote and preached to alert others to the city's danger. Each established a distinct anti-urban tradition, still honored by many who know nothing of its origin.

By background and vocation a countryman, Jefferson expressed throughout his life a strong aversion to the city and a preference for a rural way of living. "Those who labor in the earth," he wrote, "are the chosen people of God, if ever He had a chosen people; whose breasts He has made His peculiar deposit for substantial and genuine virtue." He never ceased to work for an order where "as few as possible shall be without a small portion of land. The small land-owners are the most precious portion of the state."*

Along with this partiality for an agrarian society went a vigorous dislike of "cities as sores on the body politic," places of useless luxury, corrupt wealth, and political exploitation. Cheap land and hostility to centralized urban control were two of the basic tenets of Jefferson's political philosophy.

Thoreau as the product of a small New England village and of the urban atmosphere of Cambridge and Harvard protested in a more personal, more emotional manner. Although the most explicit formulation of his antiurbanism is

[From *Landscape*, Vol. 15, No. 2, Winter 1965–66]
*Notes on the State of Virginia, ed. William Peden (Chapel Hill: University of North Carolina Press, 1955), p. 164.

Walden, the narrative of two years' withdrawal from the world of men, there is scarcely a page of his writings that does not express his opinion of city life, nor his devotion to the landscape of nature. In the essay "Walking," his final literary testament, he voices the conviction in a passage often quoted by partisans of the wilderness experience: "I wish to speak a word for nature, for absolute freedom and wildness, as contrasted with a freedom and culture merely civil— to regard man as an inhabitant, or a part and parcel of nature, rather than as a member of society."*

The influence of these two men has been to confirm a tendency marked among American intellectuals, to decry almost every aspect of life in the modern city and to praise the rural or suburban alternative. But how much does the antiurbanism of Jefferson resemble that of Thoreau? Does it in fact resemble it at all? In *The Intellectual Versus the City*† Morton and Lucia White caution us that antiurban sentiment in America had many different sources and that the city has been found wanting as either too civilized, or not civilized enough. The distinction applies to Jefferson and Thoreau; and it still separates the critics of the city into two groups.

The key passage in Jefferson's denunciation of the city and praise of the country is undoubtedly the phrase: "The country produces more virtuous citizens."‡ What he prefers to urban society is not rural solitude but rural society; the type of man he wishes to encourage as opposed to the urban cit-

The Works of Thoreau, ed. Henry Seidel Canby (Boston: Houghton Mifflin Co., 1937), p. 659.
† Cambridge: Harvard University Press and M.I.T. Press, 1962.
‡ *Notes on the State of Virginia,* p. 175.

izen, oppressed by wealth and corruption, is not simply the rural inhabitant, it is the rural citizen, an active and effective participant in the political life of his community. It is true that Jefferson held that man is more "natural" when in a rural setting, but "natural" as he used the word had little to do with "nature"—at least in its wilderness state; a "natural" man was inevitably a social or, more precisely, a political creature. The significant relationship, the relationship which fostered better men, was that between man and man. If the rural setting was to be preferred, this was chiefly because it made the relationship easier.

To Thoreau, on the other hand, the essential distinction between town and country—or, better yet, between town and wilderness—was that between society and nature; between man as a member of society and man as an inhabitant of the earth. Far from discovering virtues in the agrarian way of life, Thoreau was scarcely more tolerant of farmers than he was of city dwellers. "There is something vulgar and foul in [the gardener's] closeness to his mistress," he remarked.*

The farmer in short is guilty of a serious offense: of failing to see himself as part and parcel of nature. For to Thoreau the significant relationship is not that between man and man; it is the relationship between man and his environment.

If the distinction now appears academic, it was doubtless equally academic to those Americans of more than a century and a half ago who were looking westward to the virgin landscape where, they believed, the future of our country lay. The pioneer farmer settling the recently surveyed land of the Northwest Territory, and the trapper and woodsman

*_A Week on the Concord and Merrimac Rivers_, ed. Odell Shepard (New York: Charles Scribner's Sons, 1921), p. 37.

pushing out beyond Kentucky to cross the Mississippi, both relished their freedom from the city. Nevertheless each stood for a different kind of revolt, each stood for a different kind of nonurban America; the one Agrarian, the other Romantic; and each attitude in time made its own characteristic imprint on the national landscape.

Agrarianism was the first of the two philosophies to produce its own environment. The National Survey of 1785 was not merely inspired by Jefferson, it was a clear expression of the Jeffersonian dislike of a powerful government, centralized in cities, and the emphasis on the small rural landowner. The survey permitted and even encouraged the forming of townships with the school section in the center, townships with their own local government; but it made no provision for cities. Jefferson had tried his hand at helping design the national capital. His sketches, proposing an extensive grid with the land divided into uniform lots, were scornfully rejected by l'Enfant, who had something more monumental in mind. But aside from one or two notable exceptions—Detroit, Baton Rouge, and Indianapolis—the cities built in the United States until late in the nineteenth century all conformed to the grid system; all were Jeffersonian.

In his remarkable study of nineteenth-century city planning in America, John Reps points out that a great majority of American towns started and grew on the grid plan because of the ease of its layout in surveying, its simplicity of comprehension, and its adaptability for speculation.* These were indeed striking advantages; it is impossible to

*The Making of Urban America: A History of City Planning in the United States (Princeton: Princeton University Press, 1965), pp. 294–324.

separate the planning and growth of most towns and cities
in nineteenth-century America from land speculation. Yet
the almost universal use of the grid for towns cannot be
entirely understood without some reference to the wider
regional grid of the National Survey—which automatically
prescribed at least the main axes of any town—nor without
some reference to the American ideal. If, in terms of design,
our cities are little more than extensions of a village grid,
the village itself—except in the older parts of the country—
is in turn little more than a fragment of the regional grid:
an orderly arrangement of uniform lots frequently focussed
about a public square with no particular function and un-
varying dimensions. The block, whether in Chicago or New
Paris, Iowa, remains the basic unit, and the block is nothing
more than a specific number of independent small holdings.
For all its monotony, the Jeffersonian design has unmistak-
able Utopian traits: it is in fact the blueprint for an agrarian
equalitarian society, and it is based on the assumption that
the landowner will be active in the democratic process. The
grid system, as originally conceived, was thus a device for
the promotion of "virtuous citizens." Its survival is a testimony to the belief, once so common among Americans, in
the possibility of human perfectibility. So it was not only
logical, but appropriate, that the grid, despite its obvious
shortcomings and its abuse by speculators, should have
remained the characteristic national design for the environment. It is, to repeat, the symbol of an agrarian Utopia composed of a democratic society of small landowners.

Thoreau had no direct role in the formulation of the Romantic environment. He was however the most eloquent
American spokesman of an attitude toward the environment

first expressed many years earlier by Rousseau and his followers. No other American succeeded as well as he in translat-
ing the Romantic point of view into native terms; none put
it into practice with such consistency and fervor. Emerson's
love of nature, genuine enough, always seems to derive
from a pleasant afternoon's walk in the country. Thoreau's
derives from a total commitment to a natural, solitary way
of life.

What undoubtedly heightened his appeal was the fact
that mid-nineteenth-century America was the one modern
state where the Romantic attitude toward the environment
still had free play; where there was still room for the fron-
tiersman and also for the designer of large-scale landscapes.

It is one of the ironies of our history that the Romantic
environment remained an urban and suburban phenomenon.
Whereas the Jeffersonian concern for man as a social being
determined the character of our whole rural landscape,
the Romantic feeling for solitude and for closeness to unspoiled nature was confined to the middle-class urban citizen
on the Eastern seaboard. Of the thousands of square miles
settled during the first half of the nineteenth century, few
if any were modified or treated according to popular Romantic ideas. Only in the 1870's did it become possible to
interest the American public in the wisdom of preserving
the scenic wonders of the wilderness West.

This exclusion of Romantic environmental design from
the workaday countryside has had a fateful effect on the
profession of landscape architecture. In England, and to a
lesser degree in France and Germany, nineteenth-century
environmental design concerned itself with the country estate and with the rural scene, and it is still part of the English landscape-architectural tradition to be versed in farm

matters. But the American landscape architect, as if taking
his cue from Thoreau, can see the wider landscape only in
terms of conservation or recreation.

In its detailed description of the nineteenth-century Romantic landscape in America, Reps's book is as full a compen-
dium of so-called picturesque designs as we have ever had;
though his leaving out of the American college campus
is an unfortunate omission. They all seem to be there: Mt.
Auburn cemetery dating from as early as 1831; Alexander
Davis's Llewellyn Park of 1853; Lake Forest; Olmsted's
plans for Central Park and for Riverside. Towns, as distinguished from suburbs, are astonishingly rare in the Romantic
tradition. Not included, of course, are Downing's Hudson
Valley estates, nor the Gothic and Italianate cottages that
by the thousands bordered the tree-lined streets of mid-
nineteenth-century America.

Despite the variety of designs—cemeteries, city parks,
suburbs; despite the differences in size and in purpose, all of
them can be easily interpreted in terms of those convictions
of Thoreau. The significant relationship is never that between the buildings, or between the layout and the surrounding city; it is always that between design and terrain;
hence the contoured streets, the ingenious and often sensitive exploitation of every topographical feature; hence the
"irregular" architecture—Gothic, Swiss, Romanesque,
which, in its attempts to blend with its setting, anticipated
Frank Lloyd Wright's by a good half century. And man
seen as "part and parcel of nature rather than as a member
of society" had to have a dwelling as isolated as possible
from his neighbors and profusely planted. The assumption
that man is always striving for freedom from society,

always pining for closer contact with nature, produced the romantic suburb—and produced no towns at all. It is interesting to note that not one of the nineteenth-century Utopian or religious communities in America had any trace of Romanticism in their layout.

Yet for all its inability to understand the political side of man, despite its flirtations with primitivism, the planned environment of the Romantics represented, no less than did the Agrarian environment, a Utopian ideal. Like the Jeffersonian landscape, it assumed that in favorable surroundings man could become better, could at last be true to his real self, given a new freedom from the city. The Agrarian landscape was vast, monolithic, and without charm; the Romantic landscape was fragmented, highly self-conscious, and from the beginning identified with an urban middle-class point of view. But both were ideal landscapes, and we are not likely to see anything of the sort again. The ability, as well as the desire, to create Utopian landscapes seems to have disappeared with their demise.

It is easy to say that those earlier Utopian landscapes were rendered obsolete by changes in American society. But Utopias are not supposed to be subject to the vicissitudes of history. When one of them dies, it is for an internal reason; and our two Utopias, the Agrarian and the Romantic, died because there were no longer Utopian men to inhabit them. What justified the grid and kept it valid for almost a century was the firm belief among Americans that it was possible to produce an ideal known as the *Virtuous Citizen*; what justified the elaborate landscaping of the Romantics was the no less firmly held belief that it was possible to produce an

ideal known as *Man the Inhabitant of the Earth*. Thoreau
and Jefferson were poles apart in their definitions of human
nature but they agreed completely as to the possibility of
defining it; and, having once defined it, of creating a suitable
environment for it.

What we have lost in the last generation is this assurance
and with it the capacity—or the temerity—to contrive Utopias. It is of no use trying to resurrect the vanished forms,
beautiful though they may have been; their philosophical
justification has gone. All that we can now do is to produce
landscapes for unpredictable men where the free and democratic intercourse of the Jeffersonian landscape can somehow
be combined with the intense self-awareness of the solitary
Romantic. The existential landscape, without absolutes,
without prototypes, devoted to change and mobility and
the free confrontation of men, is already taking form around
us. It has vitality but it is neither physically beautiful nor
socially just. Our own American past has an invaluable
lesson to teach us: a coherent, workable landscape evolves
where there is a coherent definition not of man but of man's
relation to the world and to his fellow men.

The Westward-moving House

Three American Houses & the People Who Lived in Them

I. Nehemiah's Ark

Three hundred years ago one Nehemiah Tinkham, with wife
Submit Tinkham and six children, landed on the shores of
New England to establish a home in the wilderness.

Like his forefathers, Tinkham had been a small farmer.
He brought with him in addition to a few household goods
those "needful things" which a catalogue for prospective
New England planters had suggested several years before:
two hoes, two saws, two axes, hammer, shovel, spade, augers,
chisels, piercers, gimlet, and hachet. These were all he had,
these and a knowledge of certain traditional skills, necessary
not only for building a house, but for clearing and farming
new land. There were no nails on the list—nails being expensive—and no equipment for livestock.

Nehemiah soon acquired some sixty acres of virgin land
at Jerusha, a new settlement a day's journey from Boston.
He did not buy the land from a private owner, white man,
or Indian; still less did he appropriate a likely corner of the
New England forest for himself. He bought it from the Jerusha town authorities who had obtained it from the Crown,
and the town assigned him his land without giving him any
choice of location.

Nevertheless his farm was as good as his neighbors'. It
comprised three kinds of land: the smallest (and most valuable) section was the home lot, of about ten acres, that faced
the green or common and was near not only other houses
but the site of the future meetinghouse. The Massachusetts

[From *Landscape*, Vol. 2, No. 3, Spring 1953]

General Court had recently ruled that no dwelling was to
be built farther from the meetinghouse than half a mile.
The two other subdivisions of the farm were meadow and
woodland. The meadow, located in the well-watered and
protected valley, was gradually cleared of trees and planted to
wheat and oats and corn, though some of it was left untilled
for the cows which Nehemiah hoped to acquire. The woodlands on the rocky hills served to provide building materials
and fuel.

The broad axe which he had brought with him from England stood him in good stead; for though he and his neighbors had originally staked out their settlement in a thick
forest, they cleared the land so rapidly of its trees that within a decade they had to go elsewhere for wood. While this
cutting of trees lasted it concerned all men. Neighbors helped
Nehemiah fell the largest trees—the oak and pine he intended to use for his house—and he in turn helped them. All
joined forces to clear the common, to build a fence around
it to prevent livestock from straying, to build a meetinghouse and a home for the minister. The Tinkhams had to
live in a temporary half-underground shelter during the
first winter, and all that Nehemiah could do was plant two
acres of wheat—never a successful crop in New England
and from the beginning overrun by barberry—plant some
of the unfamiliar Indian corn, and set out a small apple
orchard on the home lot.

Until he died Nehemiah never grew or tasted a tomato,
an Irish potato or a sweet potato. He never tasted either tea
or coffee, and seldom tasted fresh beef or pork or lamb. The
farm eventually provided the family with flour, a few fruits
and vegetables, milk, butter, cheese, and eggs. These, together with game, made up most of their diet.

Nor did the Tinkhams possess a yoke of oxen or a work-horse until many years after they arrived in the New World. The fields which Nehemiah cultivated in spite of the many stumps were plowed for him by the one man in Jerusha who owned a plow. He harvested his wheat with a sickle, threshed it with a flail. He was fortunate to possess a crude two-wheeled cart for hauling loads, though whatever traveling he and his family did (it was little enough) was done on horseback. The few roads in the center of the village were rough and narrow; between villages there were no roads at all, merely trails through the woods.

Family and Superfamily: Had Nehemiah wanted to expand his farming activities, had he been interested in greater yields, and in selling to city markets and buying city goods in return, he would have resented these restrictions on movement and sought to improve his agricultural methods. But he was concerned first with keeping himself and his family alive, and then with maintaining an established way of life. It was a monotonous one, perhaps, but it provided him with food and clothes and shelter, and with the kind of sociability he wanted.

Poor communications with the outside world, a large degree of self-sufficiency, the pioneer custom of all men working together on certain undertakings, and lastly the grouping of all houses around the "Place for Sabbath Assembly" made for a very compact village. In our more charitable appraisals of early New England we speak of its democracy. Actually its guiding principle was something else. There was nothing particularly democratic about the social setup of proprietors, yeomen, and latecomers in descending order of importance and privilege. There was nothing democratic about the law which forbade those having less than a certain amount of money to wear expensive clothes. Nor were these latter-day backslidings from an earlier democracy; as early as 1623 it had been proposed that New England be settled by "Three sorts—Gentlemen to bear arms, handicraftsmen of all sorts, and husbandmen for tilling the ground." Likewise the Puritan Church had its hierarchy of elders, deacons, and ministers. In the Jerusha meetinghouse the higher your social position the nearer you sat to the pulpit; when Nehemiah acquired a servant she was obliged to sit in the cold gallery with the children. The right to vote, the right to live within the township, the right to speak one's mind—these were jealously controlled by law.

Yet if Jerusha was not as democratic as a modern American town it had a quality which the modern town has lost. It was a kind of superfamily, more like the highest stage in a domestic hierarchy than the smallest unit of a nation, as it is now. Nehemiah found Jerusha a good substitute for the rural society he had left behind. He had never traveled much in England, and his father and grandfather had traveled even less. To generations of Tinkhams, family and village had been almost interchangeable terms. Nehemiah had been related to most of his neighbors in the Old World and had shared customs and traditions with them all. The people who came to Jerusha came, of course, from different places and from different walks of life, but like the Tinkhams they were all of them homesick, not so much for the safety and comfort of England as for the superfamily they had known. What could take the place of that? Nothing so impersonal as a social contract; what they created instead was the domestic village with its established hierarchy and its working together on a common task.

Certainly the most obvious symbols of the urge for a super-family were God the stern Father, the Jerusha meeting-house as a sort of superparlor where the family gathered for prayers, and the genealogical enthusiasm which still possesses New England. But the individual house was scarcely less important, and Nehemiah hastened to build his family as good a house as he could in order to reproduce still another aspect of the traditional background. The completed article was naturally reminiscent of the house he had known in England. It was of wood, of course, much of it unseasoned, with a stone foundation, and it was two stories high with a third story or attic under a steeply pitched roof.

The House: As Anthony Garvan has pointed out in his *Architecture and Town Planning in Colonial Connecticut* * the early builders (Nehemiah included) used as a basic measurement in their houses the sixteen-foot bay—a span originally adopted in England because it was wide enough to house two teams of oxen. In America this was modified to the extent that almost every dimension in the colonial house was divisible by eight—or half a bay. Another sign of Nehemiah's conservatism was the manner in which he built the house. The frame of oak which he laboriously constructed with the simplest of tools was a heavy and intricate piece of carpentry —unlike anything we see in contemporary construction. To quote Garvan: "Such frames . . . not only carried the whole weight of the building but were also mortised and tenoned together so that they withstood any horizontal thrust of the elements. . . . The task of the frame was to carry the weight of the roof and ridgepole, not just to resist their outward thrust."

* New Haven: Yale University Press, 1951.

Thus Nehemiah's house was built to last, built to be inflexible, built to carry a load, and not built for easy alteration or enlargement—like his theology, perhaps.

He never painted the house, nor sought to adorn it, but the passage of years has given it softness and beauty, and now we hear persons admire its functionalism. Hugh Morrison remarks in his *Early American Architecture** that the seventeenth-century builder was so far from being functionally minded that he never thought of inserting sheathing between the frame and the outside clapboards; never realized that the huge chimney was inefficient, or that the lighting in the house was atrociously bad. He never realized that the old-fashioned frame he took such pains with was needlessly slow and difficult to make.

The plan of the house was equally nonfunctional as we understand the term. The ground floor had two main rooms: a combination living room-work room-kitchen with a large fireplace, and a parlor, also with a fireplace. The parlor was reserved for important guests and family religious observances. Between these two a flight of stairs led to the two bedrooms where the family slept, and above these, reached by a ladder, was the attic, where slept the servant. There were in addition several outbuildings, including a barn, all near the house. Outside the back door there was a small garden chiefly devoted to vegetables and herbs, but containing a few flowers as well. The lawn which we always think of as in front of the Colonial house did not exist; a rail fence surrounded the place and kept out cows. The appearance of the house was forlorn bleak and graceless; its windows were small, the proportion of the rooms ungainly, and the furnishings scanty and of necessity crude. But Nehemiah and

* New York: Oxford University Press, 1952.

his wife Submit found little to criticize in it. It was solid,
practical, and defensible against Indian assaults. If anyone
dared mention its discomforts Nehemiah quoted Romans 5:3.

Meetinghouse as Parlor : We cannot judge the house without knowing what functions it was supposed to serve and
what functions it relegated to some other establishment.
We are no more entitled to speak of the gloom of the Tinkhams' existence simply because their house lacked facilities
for conviviality than a foreigner would be entitled to speak of
the idleness of modern American existence because our houses
do not contain places of work. Nehemiah's home cannot be
understood without some understanding of the importance
of the meetinghouse, for the one complemented the other.
If the dwelling sheltered the economic and biological functions of domestic life in Jerusha, the social and cultural functions belonged to the meetinghouse. That perhaps is why
Nehemiah was almost as attached to the square edifice on the
common as he was to his own home; not because he had
helped build it with his own hands, not because he thought
it beautiful, but because it was an essential part of his life.

It was school and forum for the discussion of civic affairs;
it was his barracks and the place where he stored his weapons
and ammunition. It was the spot for community gatherings
and celebrations. Most important of all it was the image of the
kind of world order that Nehemiah believed in. Here and
here alone he felt that he was occupying his ordained place
in the scheme of existence, even if that place was humble.
He did not enjoy sitting for two hours in a cold building
while the Reverend Jethro Tipping expounded the Significance of the Tenth Horn of the Beast, but he believed
that all was well while he did so. Dozing off during the

exegesis he saw the world as an enduring and majestic pyramid, an orderly succession of ranks—yeoman, husbandmen, squires; elders, deacons, ministers; heathen, gentile, elect—each one indispensable to the solidity of the structure, and helping to bear the weight of the crowning stone. Apt as it was to thinking in allegories, Nehemiah's fancy saw the same spirit manifest in the landscape around him, in the ascending orders of woodland, meadow, and home lot; in unredeemed wilderness, settlement, and meetinghouse on the common.

In this hierarchical view of the world he was a child of his age. What distinguished him, however, from his cousins in Europe was his conviction that the order could and should be simplified. Some of the steps in the pyramid ought to be eliminated, as it were, for communication between the highest and the lowest to be more direct and certain. If this world was but a preparation for the next (and the Reverend Jethro Tipping assured him that it was) men should organize it simply and efficiently. And in fact Nehemiah and his fellow colonists had already done this so well that in the eyes of their Old-World contemporaries they passed for revolutionaries.

The Hostile Environment: Nevertheless, Jerusha was aware that it was only a small beleaguered island of holiness in the midst of a hostile country. Almost within gunshot of the meetinghouse was an unredeemed wilderness inhabited by savages. A variety of factors prevented Nehemiah from venturing very far or very often into this hinterland. His farming methods were too primitive; labor was too scarce for him to exploit all the land he owned—much less acquire more. The absence of roads made settlement difficult in the more remote parts and again prevented him from selling to distant towns. Furthermore, neither he nor his friends were adventurous spirits; they were slow to adopt new ways and new ideas, since the old ones were backed by unimpeachable authority. Remembering the cultivated countryside they had left in England, they were appalled by the lawlessness of the New-World environment. No doubt much of this fear of the environment came from the hardships of pioneer life.

But in fact later generations of American pioneers had little or none of this hostility to nature; the sentiment was largely confined to Nehemiah and his time. What helped confirm it and make it almost an article of faith was the habit the early colonists had of comparing themselves to the Children of Israel in the Wilderness. "Thou hast brought a vine out of Egypt. Thou hast cast out the heathen and planted it." Such was the biblical inspiration of the motto of Connecticut and of the state seal adopted in 1644. How great is the contrast between such an emblem and those of the western pioneer states of two centuries later, with their rising suns and optimistic plowmen!

It is possible to interpret the landscape of Jerusha as the expression of pioneer economic conditions. The village centered on the common and meetinghouse, the houses turning their backs on the woodlands, the small fields surrounded by fences and walls—these are certainly traits of a subsistence economy and of a society compelled to think in terms of self-defense. Even the nonexistent lions and the soporific ferns, in one form or another, are part of every pioneer environment. But we should not forget that Nehemiah thought of himself not as a pioneer but as an exile, that he strove throughout his life not only for security but for holiness, and his interests never wandered very far from that font of holiness, the meetinghouse. He never aspired to much more than establishing as firmly as he could a superdomestic order. He closed his eyes on this vale of tears in 1683, satisfied until his latest breath that two things at least were permanent: his own identity (which would rise in the flesh on the Day of Judgment) and the indestructible, unalterable house which he bequeathed to his widow Submit.

It was lucky he died when he did. Had he lived to see his grandson Noah come of age he would have witnessed the beginning of the end of the old order. Noah was one of the first in Jerusha to start speculating in land values. He realized that there was no longer room near the common for more houses and that newcomers were not eager to belong to the church community; they were willing to live far away. It was Noah who persuaded the town selectmen to build roads into the forest five miles distant, and he made a substantial profit selling off some of his grandfather's unused woodland.

His was not so well-behaved a world as Nehemiah's, but it was more extensive. It included the West Indies and Virginia and many new towns and frontier farms off by themselves in distant clearings. It included men who went about on horseback preaching a road to salvation much shorter and simpler than the one Nehemiah had so earnestly followed, and others who talked of a more direct relationship between people and government. Noah built himself a three-story house and furnished the parlor with mahogany and silver. The old house, now gray and in poor repair, was lived in by one of Noah's aunts. She prided herself on being loyal to the old ways, but she complained that the house was cramped, and put in larger windows on the ground floor; and she always referred to New England as home.

II. Pliny's Homestead

The first time a member of the Tinkham family built a house outside of New England was when Pliny Tinkham moved West a little over a century ago, and homesteaded near Illium, Illinois.

Pliny was young to be married and the father of three children, and young (his parents thought) to be going so far from Jerusha. But though he was not rich he had much more to start with than his ancestors had had two centuries earlier. He needed much more; he intended to farm on a larger and more complicated scale. Aside from money, Pliny and his wife Matilda took little with them, having been advised to buy whatever they needed near their destination. When they finally arrived at Illium they had bought (in addition to the same set of tools that Nehemiah had for pioneering) a team of horses, a yoke of oxen, a milch cow, a wagon, a plow, a pitchfork, a scythe—and ten pounds of nails. These were the articles listed as necessary in the farmers' and emigrants' handbook which Pliny consulted.

Pioneering in the Plains: Nehemiah, it will be remembered, had been assigned land by the township; land comprising three different kinds of terrain. Pliny, though no judge of prairie real estate, was obliged to choose the land he wanted and to bargain for it. He finally bought 120 acres from a man who had acquired it as a speculation, had done nothing to improve it, and now wanted to move even farther West. It was excellent land: gently rolling prairie with very rich soil; it contained a small amount of woodland and was about ten miles north of Illium on what would some day be a road. The nearest neighbor was a mile away.

Like Nehemiah, Pliny built a temporary shelter for the family first of all; only he built it out of logs and thus made it larger and more comfortable than the first underground Tinkham shelter. He did not have to cut down many trees to clear his land, for most of it was clear already, but he did have to cut them down for the log cabin, for a barn for the livestock and for fences to keep the animals from wandering across the prairie. He soon saw that wood was not to be wasted in southern Illinois; there was too little of it. Again like his ancestor, Pliny hastened to plant the fields he had prepared; but instead of planting for family needs he planted twenty acres to wheat—in order to have a cash crop as soon as he could.

In many ways his pioneering was easier than that of Nehemiah. Pliny had no "hostiles" to deal with. The land was fertile and open, and he had the tradition of adaptability and self-reliance in a new country. He had a growing market not too far away, and a place where he could always buy to satisfy his needs. And then, finally, he and Matilda were optimistic and adventurous; the very fact that the purchase of the land had been a kind of speculation encouraged them to look at the whole enterprise of homesteading as speculative, for in a pinch they could always sell out and begin again.

On the other hand, life during the first years was often harsh. Matilda had a recipe for bread made of powdered beechwood and another for salad made of young pine needles, both to be used in times of near-famine. She found herself having to practice a variety of domestic skills which the people of Jerusha had either never known or had been able to delegate to specialists within the village: the making of candles and soap and dyes, of sugar from corn and yeast from milk. She had to tend a much larger vegetable garden than Submit Tinkham had ever seen, and preserve vegetables that Submit had never heard of. She had to nurse a family and keep it well according to methods which were scientific if rudimentary, whereas Submit had merely relied on traditional quackery and semi-magic formulae or had turned to any neighbor who had had medical experience. As for Pliny, he was not only farmer, carpenter, mason, engineer, and blacksmith, he was also veterinarian, hunter and trapper, experimental agriculturalist, and merchant.

Moreover, the Tinkhams of Illinois were from the beginning much more on their own than the Tinkhams of Massachusetts. What neighbors they had were friendly, but they were remote and few. The Tinkham dwelling was several miles from Illium (and a good distance across prairie mud from the road leading to Illium) and once Pliny reached the town he discovered that no one there felt any responsibility for his welfare, spiritual or physical. The banker, the storekeeper, the shipper were all eager to do business with him, but they were not much interested in his personal problems. There was not one church in Illium; there were three. One of the ministers came out to see the Tinkhams, led a a prayer, left a few tracts, and never came back. The population of Illium was constantly growing and changing. The rumor of a new railroad, of a packing plant, of a new county seat sent half of them scurrying elsewhere. In spite of his spending a good deal of time at the courthouse and in the bank, and of attending every fair, Pliny always felt like an outsider in the town.

Flight from the Village : To his forefather such a feeling would have been almost too humiliating to bear, but Pliny was a different person. He needed a different society, a dif-

ferent economy, and a different landscape, and he had left
New England because he knew that he needed them. The
reason given by the Tinkham tribe for the young man's
defection was that there was more money to be made in
farming out West, which was true, and that the old farm was
exhausted after two hundred years of cultivation, which it
was not. They also blamed the railroads, the cheap land, the
growth of the large cities—everything except themselves.
But the fact is Pliny had rebelled against the old-fashioned
farming methods of his father and against the old-fashioned
domestic tyranny. The elder Tinkham, obsessed by the an-
cestral craving for security and solvency, and, like his ancestors, indifferent to the promise of wealth, had steadfastly
refused either to enlarge the farm or improve it in keeping
with new ideas. What had been good enough for Nehemiah
was good enough for him. Furthermore, he firmly believed
that as father, as representative of God in the home, he always knew best, that he was the apex of the established domestic order. He treated Pliny as a child of ten. Thus, when
Pliny moved West it was not so much in search of easy
money as in flight from the Old Testament household, the
old self-sufficient economy; in a way it might be said he was
fleeing the New England village: common, meetinghouse,
and all.

It was natural that the landscape which he and the other
fugitives created in the West should have been in many respects the direct opposite of the landscape they had known
as children. Instead of the cluster of farmhouses around the
church, there were farmhouses scattered far and wide across
the prairie; instead of the land being fairly and equally ap-
portioned by a benevolent authority, it was bought in the
open market; and instead of the superfamily life of the New

England village there was no village life at all. It was as if
Pliny (like his remote ancestor) had set out in his turn to
eliminate a few more steps in the hierarchy, some of the
barriers between himself and immediate experience. Parents,
clergy, aristocracy, township in the old sense were all abol-
ished. And the chief artificer of the landscape was no longer
the community but the individual. The independence that
Pliny felt was expressed in a popular song:

> *I have lawns, I have bowers*
> *I have fruits, I have flowers*
> *The lark is my morning alarmer.*

> So jolly boys, now,
> Here's God speed the plow
> Long life and success to the farmer!

The Functional House, 1860 : Most significant of all of
Pliny's creations was his house, for it incorporated more
revolutionary features than had any previous house in America. He placed it on a height in the center of the farm, where
the air was fresh and the view wide, though he built at some
distance from the highway and out of sight of his neighbors.
He and Matilda agreed that their house should be built primarily for the use of the family rather than for display or
entertaining, and that it should be designed so that if need
arose it could easily be sold. This was the advice that every
homeowner gave them, and it was in keeping with the speculative attitude they both unconsciously retained from the
very first days on the farm. But that was only the beginning.
After reading several useful handbooks on building, Pliny
and Matilda decided that their home should be a place which
could be added to in the future as the family grew and as

they put aside more money; they planned for rooms which could be used as bedrooms now and later as storerooms, they planned for sliding doors which could divide a room in two.

A house with a flexible plan, a house designed so sensibly that it could be used by one family and then sold to another—a house, in short, that adjusted itself willingly to that outward thrust which Nehemiah's house had resisted so stoutly—was in itself a totally new concept. Equally new was the way Pliny built it. He abandoned the time-honored frame construction of his ancestors—and (significantly enough) the traditional dimensions based on the bay and the half bay—and used the latest method, the so-called balloon construction. Balloon construction is actually the type of construction we now use in every frame house in this country, but it was invented only a little over a century ago. Its principle, as Giedion defines it in *Space, Time, and Architecture* "involves the substitution of thin plates and studs, running the entire height of the building and held together only by nails, for the ancient and expensive method of construction with mortised and tenoned joints. To put together a house, like a box," he adds, "using only nails—this must have seemed utterly revolutionary to carpenters."* But to Pliny, who never prided himself on being a radical innovator, it was the logical procedure. It called for cheap and plentiful nails, and these he had.

So the house was inexpensive and fast to build, and it was larger, better-lighted, and more convenient than the house in Jerusha. Its rooms were numerous, and whereas Nehemiah had thought chiefly in terms of the social function of each room—one for the family, one for ceremonies, one for

* Third edition (Cambridge: Harvard University Press, 1954), p. 345.

the servant and so on, Pliny thought in terms of domestic or practical function: kitchen, milkroom, pantry, livingroom, bedrooms and of course a piazza. Just as he had promised, it was a house designed entirely for family life and not for show. What was the spiritual center of this dwelling? In Jerusha it had been the formal parlor with its Bible and hearth. But because of the scarcity of wood around Illium, and because of the more sensible arrangement of the rooms, Pliny had only Franklin burners and a cookstove; two fires sufficed to heat the entire establishment. All that remained of the hearth was an open Franklin burner in the living-room (or sitting room, as Matilda called it); and a small collection of books for family reading. Whittier and Long-fellow and *Household Words* took their places alongside the Bible.

To say that the most important room in the Tinkham house was dedicated to family gatherings rather than to cere-monial occasions is to say that the house was designed for social self-sufficiency. None of the previous Tinkhams ever had so complete and independent a homelife as Pliny. This was chiefly because the house had to take the place of the church and meetinghouse and school—and sometimes even the tavern. Weddings, funerals, burials, business deals, holi-days gave it an importance that no Tinkham dwelling had ever had before or ever had afterwards. It expanded to include almost every aspect of country living; it represented in its way the golden age of the American home.

The Functional Farm: The farm which Pliny operated was not only larger than the one in Jerusha, it was far more effi-cient. Nehemiah had done everything by hand except haul stone and wood, and plow. On the farm near Illium every phase of the process of raising corn, except for husking, was done by horse power—and this long before the Civil War. Nehemiah had not owned one piece of farm machinery; Pliny had wagons, plows, cultivators, and harrows; and after ten years, when the roads had been improved, he acquired a buggy.

Nehemiah had chiefly sought to satisfy his family needs from the proceeds of the farm, and as long as the family needs remained pretty much the same year after year, he saw no point in increasing the size of the farm or its yield. Pliny, on the contrary, gave up after the first two years any attempt to provide for the family in the traditional way; why raise sheep and spin wool and weave and dye and sew, when the railroad was bringing in ready-made clothes from the East? So he devoted more and more of his land to a cash crop— corn—which he could easily dispose of for ready money.

Once embarked on commercial farming, Pliny no longer had any reason for limiting the size of his farm; no matter how much he raised he could always sell it—or so it seemed; and as a result the farm started to expand. He bought other small farms, leased land, sold land, cleared land until he never quite knew how much he controlled. The expanding farm went hand in hand with the expanding house. Nehemiah had never changed the shape of his fields, bordered as they were with stone walls and each distinct as to soil and slope from the others. But Pliny, using wooden fences, could change his fields at will, and as he acquired large horse-drawn machinery he consolidated many small fields into a few big ones. Again, the flexible plan of the farm paralleled the flexible plan of the house.

From the beginning, Pliny had never seen the wisdom of having a diversity of land; he had naturally wanted as much of the best as he could afford to buy, and a uniform topography was certainly most practical for a uniform crop. He never had any of Nehemiah's feeling that even the worst and least productive patch of land served some inscrutable purpose in an overall scheme. He spent much time and thought trying to modify the farm and increase its yield, thus making it impersonal and efficient, and easier to sell to another corn farmer.

It is unfortunately true that Pliny robbed the farm of variety and human association, and made it look more like a place of work than a traditional landscape; but it would be wrong to say that he did not love it. He probably never had that dim sense which Nehemiah had of being in partnership with a particular piece of earth. Pliny was indeed a strict and arbitrary master. Nevertheless he and Matilda and the children felt another kind of love which their colonial ancestor had never known. They enjoyed what in those days was called the grandiose spectacle of Nature. Pliny rode and hunted and fished in the remoter parts of the countryside, his children played in the woodlot and in the streams, and around the house Matilda planted a grove of locust trees and a romantic garden of wild flowers and vines. They belonged to a generation which believed that only good could come from close contact with Nature; like Thoreau they regarded Man as a part of Nature, rather than as a member of society. Never a church-goer but always inclined to piety, Pliny was fond of saying that God could be worshipped in the great out-of-doors without the assistance of a preacher. As one of the emigrant handbooks put it (no doubt to reassure those pioneers who had always kept up their church attendance at home): "The church-going bell is not heard within his wild domain, nor organ, nor anthem, nor choir. But there is music in the deep silence. . . . He is indeed within a Temple not made with hands."

The Family as a Natural Society · It is hard to realize that there was ever a time when such sentiments were new. But a century ago they not only represented a fresh approach to the environment, but a greatly simplified religious experience. Pliny loved the world of unspoiled nature for the same reason Nehemiah had dreaded it: it afforded him a direct and unimpeded glimpse of reality. Nehemiah had preferred to retain a hierarchy of Scripture and clergy between himself and the source of wisdom. Pliny liked to imagine that God was separated from him by little more than the thin veil of appearances.

The same sentiment inspired his concept of the ideal homelife. Remembering his family in Jerusha, forcibly subordinated to Old Testament law and parental authority, he chose to think of the household on the farm at Illium as a happy group of free individuals held together by common interests and affections, a beautifully natural society, independent of the outside world and unspoiled by artifice.

As he grew older Pliny had from time to time an uneasy suspicion that the house and the farm were no longer quite in harmony. The old domestic crafts had long since been abandoned, and increased contact with the national economy, increased dependence on hired help and semi-professional skills, all tended to disrupt the ancient unity and self-sufficiency. But until his death in 1892 Pliny looked upon the homestead as the source of every virtue he admired: frugality and simplicity and independence. The free American farmer was the noblest of men, and to think of leaving the farm was to risk losing his identity. His solution to every problem, domestic or agricultural, was "add a new room" or "buy some more land." He insisted on a home burial (the last in the county) as a sort of final investment in the land, a final planting. He had no doubt that the proceeds would be profitable to everyone.

He never dreamt that his grandchildren would desert the place as soon as he vanished. They did, however. They could no longer enjoy the kind of life Pliny had arranged for them. They wanted less routine, more excitement; they took no pride in owning a large farm and having little cash, and they were bored with their identity as independent landowners. They rapidly went their several ways and the farm was eventually acquired by an immigrant with fourteen children who raised onions, acres and acres of onions.

Pliny's way of life died with him, but Pliny's ghost, and Pliny's home continue to haunt us. To many urban Americans they still embody a national ideal. Thanksgiving in Pliny's kitchen, fishing in the ole swimmin' hole on Pliny's farm, Pliny himself behind a team of plow horses now advertise beer and refrigerators and "Free Enterprise." But the Tinkham family (who ought to have known what they were leaving behind, and why they left it) have long since moved on, and not all the persuasion of advertising copy writers and politicians can make them return to the farm near Illium.

III. Ray's Transformer

The latest Tinkham house is not yet finished. It is being built at Bonniview, Texas, by Ray Tinkham, who hopes to have it completed sometime next spring.

Meanwhile, he and Shirley and the two children, Don

and Billie-Jean, are still living out on the ranch with the Old
Man. The Old Man, though a widower, does not want to leave
the story-and-a-half frame house with its broad veranda that
he built at the turn of the century. It is set in the midst of the
cottonwoods which he and his wife planted, thinking of the
grove of locusts around the house in Illinois. So he will stay
there until he dies. Ray and he have a written partnership
agreement by which the Old Man feeds a certain number
of steers, while Ray manages the farm. It used to be a cattle
ranch, but having discovered a vast underground supply
of water Ray now plans to raise large crops of wheat or
cotton or sorghum or castor beans, depending on the market.
For the last month the bulldozers and earthmovers and cat-
erpillars of a contracting firm have been levelling part of the
range, contouring slopes, building irrigation ditches and
storage tanks, and installing pumps. "You'd never know the
place," the Old Man says as he looks at the brand-new geo-
metrical landscape. He often wonders how the venture is
being financed—as well he might, for Ray Tinkham has little
cash, and there is hardly a farm credit institution, public or
private, that is not somehow involved. But Ray is not worried, and the Old Man has confidence in his son.

Now is the slack time of the year, and every afternoon
the two men and Ray's boy Don, and once in a while a
neighbor, go to work on Ray's new house. It is being built
out of the best grade cement block, brought by truck some
two hundred miles, and it is to be absolutely the last word
in convenience and modern construction. It is to be flat
roofed and one story high, with no artistic pretensions, but
intelligently designed. It is located on a barren and treeless
height of land on the outskirts of town. It has city water
of course as well as city gas. Ray bought four lots on

speculation when he came out of the Navy. From the large picture window in the living room there will be a view of prairie and a glimpse of a strange rock formation in the valley below. It will even be possible to see a corner of the ranch twelve miles away; the dust being raised by the cater-pillars is very visible when the wind is right.

Planning the House : Twelve miles is an ideal distance. It means that Ray can get out to the headquarters (as he calls the old ranch house) in less than twenty minutes in his pick-up, and leave his work far behind him at the end of the day. If the young Tinkhams were to continue to live out on the ranch the children would have to travel by bus to the new consolidated school in Bonniview, and even then miss the supervised after-school play period. As it is they will be able to walk the four blocks to school, and their mother will be near her friends after the daily trip to the supermarket and the food locker. She will be able to drop in on any of them for coffee. Ray approves all these arrangements and is count-ing the days until he and Shirley and the children have their own house.

He has even put up a rough frame where the picture win-dow will eventually be, and Shirley never tires of looking out of it, over the vacant prairie and the strange rock for-mation below. Ray, who is a graduate of an agricultural college, pretends that he knows nothing about planning a house and leaves almost every decision to his wife. A very wise move, for she has not only pored over every home dec-orating magazine available, she has practical ideas of her own. She wants the house to be informal and not too big; easy to take care of, easy to live in, cheerful and comfortable. Styles and periods mean nothing to her, and since the place will be adequately heated by gas she suggests that they save money by doing without a fireplace and chimney. She apparently knows the role the house can be expected to play in the life of the family, regardless of the role it might have played in the past. She knows that once in the new home the children will spend most of their time elsewhere and receive little of their upbringing in the house or from her. She will give them bed and breakfast, send them off to school and in the late afternoon they will return in time to eat, having learned from their teachers how to sew, how to be polite, how to brush their teeth, how to buy on the installment plan—knowledge which Shirley herself acquired (after a fashion) from her parents. Eventually the two children will leave the house altogether, and their mother has already decided what to do with their bedrooms when that happens.

Ray, as a matter of principle, has never transacted any of his work at home, and even leaves the ranch books with an expert accountant in Bonniview. For the new house Shirley plans a small dressing room off the garage where her husband can wash and change his clothes after work. It is not that she feels that the home should be devoted exclusively to her interests, though the family recognizes her as the boss; indeed she is just as eager as anyone to reduce the functions of the house and to make it a convenience rather than a responsibility.

She wants as many labor-saving devices as they can afford; she wants to have an electric dishwasher, and a garbage disposal unit, and incinerator built into the wall of the kitchen; she wants thermostat heat control and air-conditioning. She wants an automatic washing machine. Confronted with these demands and with Shirley's reluctance to have a lawn or a vegetable garden—"Who would water it?"—or a separate

dining room for company—"Just another room to take care
of and more people to feed."—Ray is tempted to ask what
she expects to do with her leisure. But he knows the answer;
actually she will be lucky to have two free hours a day; and
he himself thinks leisure—time spent away from routine
work—a very desirable thing, though he cannot say precisely
why, and he knows that Shirley is not lazy, that the house
should not monopolize her time. It is not important enough
to any of them for that.

The Functions of the Home : He is right. It would be absurd
to talk of the new Tinkham house as an institution, when it
represents so little of permanent significance. What connection, for instance, can it possibly have with the process
of earning the daily bread when it is twelve miles distant
from the place of work? Its educational function will grow
slighter every year; even homework has been done away with
in the Bonniview public schools, and discipline is largely left
to the teachers. Whoever falls sick goes to the hospital, for
modern medical practice involves the use of complicated
technical equipment. What social prestige is attached to the
house that Ray is building? Neither he nor Shirley gave any
thought to social or snobbish factors when they chose its
site; convenience was all that mattered. They will sooner
or later clamor for a paved road in front, but expensive and
time-consuming landscaping they both consider superfluous
until they know how long they will continue to live there.
Although the Tinkhams have social ambitions like everyone
else in Bonniview they instinctively know that their standing
depends more on the organizations they belong to, the car
they drive, the clothes they wear, than on their house and its
furnishings.

They have no illusions as to the permanence of the establishment they are about to set up. It does not occur to them
that they will spend their old age in the house, much less
that the children will inherit it and live in it after they have
gone. As for the kind of family life that the Old Man knew
back East in Illinois—reading out loud together, Bible instruction, games, large holiday dinners, winter evenings in
the sitting room and so forth—the very mention of it makes
Shirley impatient. The only time *her* family spends its leisure together—except for rapid meals—is when they are out
in the car. And when the children do stay home they go to
their separate rooms and watch their favorite programs on
their portable TV's. The Tinkham house will have no provision for a permanent library of books, for a common literary heritage; an unending stream of newspapers and mag-
azines scarely ever read, will pass through the living room.
The Old Man regrets that the children have no religious
instruction; has Shirley ever tried reading the Bible to them?
"For pity's sake, Dad! Ray and me never go to church, so
why should the kids?"

If such is to be the economic and social and cultural status
—or lack of status—of the new Tinkham home, what will
actually distinguish it from a motel—which indeed it promises to resemble at least on the outside? Chiefly this: it is
the one place where certain experiences, certain external
energies are collected and transformed for the benefit of the
group. This is clear in the design of the house itself: it is
consciously planned to "capture" the sun, the breezes, the
view, to filter the air, the heat, the light—even the distance,
through the picture window, transforming them and making
them acceptable to everyone. The kitchen is essentially a
marvelous electric range which transforms raw or semi-raw

materials into food; the livingroom is the television set
which transforms electronic impulses into entertainment;
the dressingroom transforms Ray from a workingman into
a different person. The whole house exists not to create some
thing new but to transform four separate individuals into a
group—though only for a few hours at a time.

In a word, the Tinkham house is to be a transformer,
and the property of transformers is that they neither increase nor decrease the energy in question but merely
change its form. There is no use inquiring what this house
will retain from the lives of its inhabitants, or what it
will contribute to them. It imposes no distinct code of
behavior or set of standards; it demands no loyalty which
might be in conflict with loyalty to the outside world. No
one will be justified in talking about the "tyranny" of the
Tinkham home, or of its ingrowing otherworldly qualities.
Neither of the children will ever associate it with repression
or wax sentimental at the thought of the days back in the
Bonniview house. But still, it serves its purposes. It filters
the crudities of nature, the lawlessness of society and produces an atmosphere of temporary well-being where vigor
can be renewed for contact with the outside.

The Function of the Farm: It is no doubt significant that
the house should be deliberately located at some distance
from the farm and that it should have no connection with
the farm setup. There are definite similarities, however,
between the farm which Ray is creating and the house still
under construction. Both of them, of course, disregard traditional form and layout, and the landscape which Ray will
eventually produce will be as functional and as unencum-
bered as the house he is building. But how does he think of

his farm? Does he, like Nehemiah, think of it as a fragment
of creation which he is to redeem, support himself from,
and pass on to his progeny? Or like Pliny, as an expanding
organism, the victory of one individual over Nature? Does
he look upon its produce as God's reward for work well and
piously done, or as part of a limitless bounty given by a
benevolent Nature to those who understand and obey her
laws? Neither; Ray is the first of the Tinkhams to doubt
the unending profusion of Nature, the first of ten generations
to believe that the farm can and should produce much more
than it has in the past, that much energy now being wasted
can be put to use. Nehemiah, who saved every penny and
never contracted a debt without examining his soul before-
hand, would deny that Ray had any sense of economy;
he turns in his grave at the thought of the mortgages and
pledges and indebtedness and of the small balance in the
Bonniview bank.

But Ray knows something that Nehemiah never knew
and Pliny never quite grasped: that *work* and *time* and *money*
are interchangeable, and that the farm serves only to transform each of these several kinds of energy into another.
What does this knowledge of Ray's imply? Nehemiah was
aware that his occasional small farm surplus could be converted into shillings and pence, but he never put those shillings back into the farm. Pliny, who disposed of most of his
produce on the market, knew that in order to get money out
of a farm you had to put money into it. Yet he never calculated the worth of his own labor or that of his sons, never
kept account of the milk and eggs and meat the family took.
He refused to make a distinction between the family and
the farm; they belonged together. Finally it never occurred
to him to expect the cost of certain improvements to be

balanced by greater yields or lower overhead. If the price of corn was low, why bother to spend money on fertilizer? The farm, like the family, was not to be treated in terms of dollars and cents.

On the other hand, Ray is organizing his farm along entirely different lines. As he sees it, it is to be an instrument for the prompt and efficient conversion of natural energy in the form of chemical fertilizer or water or tractor fuel or man-hours or whatever into energy in the form of cash or further credit—into economic energy, in a word. There are still a few old-fashioned ranchers near Bonniview who accuse young Tinkham of being money minded. Farming, after all, is a way of life, they say, and science and new ideas can be carried too far. They think that if he had not gone to agricultural college but had served an apprenticeship with his father on the ranch he would be more respectful of the old order.

The Identity of House and Farm: Ray dismisses these criticisms as beside the point. He did not invent this kind of farming all by himself; his chief contribution is a willingness to accept certain definite trends. Labor is expensive and hard to get, so he has to mechanize and streamline his operations. Mechanization is expensive on a small irregular farm, so he has to expand and gamble on the results. The market fluctuates, so he must be ready to adjust the farm to other more profitable operations, or to sell it at a good price and get out. The farm is not a self-supporting economic unit, it depends on the outside world, so he must be assured of good roads and efficient transportation. Thus the new farm reproduces many of the characteristics of the new house: labor-saving devices, efficient and simplified layout,

adaptability to and anticipation of change, and dependence
on the proximity of a complex economy, on markets, super
or otherwise. Like every other new house in rural America,
the Tinkhams', in materials, method of construction and
location, has no organic relationship to its environment—
weather or topography or soil. The Tinkham farm is of
course something of a new departure, and its efficiency is
yet to be proved. But it too is pretty much detached from
the semi-arid Southwestern landscape which surrounds it.
Ray has changed the topography in no uncertain manner;
his abundance of water for irrigation amounts to a change in
the climate, and the soil—which even his father had always
thought to be a constant factor—is being altered and improved in a variety of effective ways. Nothing more need be
said of the infinitesimal cultural role which the home plays
in the Tinkham family, but it is worth noting that the farm
is, if anything, even less productive on that score. In the
days when the Old Man ran the ranch and had several families of workers living on the place, there was such a thing
as a sense of unity among them all, and there was a distinc-
tive way of life. Ray's few workers are paid well and treated
well but they check in and out like factory hands and think
of their boss as an impersonal entity known as the Tinkham
Land Development Company. And in fact Ray pays himself
a salary as manager.

Two paint ponies stand in the corral waiting for Don and
Billie-Jean to ride them. Once the farm is in operation they
will be ridden on weekends only and in certain prescribed
areas. Ray has made it clear that the farm is no place for
Don to play at being farmer or rancher: "If he wants to
learn the business he'll have to go to agricultural college
the way I did, and study chemistry and engineering and

accounting." Don, however, at present wants to be a jet
pilot.

The ranch will not take every one of Ray's working hours.
He hopes in time to be able to leave it to look after itself,
not merely overnight but for weeks on end, while he and
Shirley and the children take winter vacations in California.
He even dreams of having a small business in town to keep
himself occupied. At present there are only two operations
which he will delegate to no one: the preparing of the soil
and planting of the seed, and the investment of the financial
proceeds. The harvesting of the crop he has already contracted out to an itinerant crew which has its own machinery,
and for several months of the year the Old Man's steers will
be turned out into the stubble. In a sense all that interests
Ray are the first process and the last—the energy which goes
into the soil in the planting and fertilizing, and the energy
which comes out of it in the form of money. How can he
and the rest of the family help but think of the new farm as
essentially an impersonal and inflexible instrument of transformation? How can they help but be indifferent to the traditional aspects of farming? The farm at Bonniview is not and
cannot be a way of life. It is not even negotiable property
(since Ray can scarely be said to own it); it is a process, a
process by which grass is converted into beef, nitrogen into
wheat, dollars into gasoline and back into dollars.

Ray's Identity : It would probably be fair to say that Ray
is not a farmer at all, any more than his house is a farm-
house. Ray would be the first to agree. Nevertheless there
is a bond between him and the land that cannot be entirely
overlooked. He himself is subject to the same forces (however defined) which have modified so drastically the concept

of the farm. For one thing, Ray's identity like the identity
of the land, has become alarmingly mobile and subject to
rapid change. His remote ancestor Nehemiah (of whom he
has never even heard) remained true to his identity of yeoman throughout his life—and even died believing he would
some day rise again intact in every particular. But for some
reason, Ray is leery of any kind of permanent label. He will
not call himself a farmer, for instance; he says he is en-
gaged in farming. And who knows what he may be doing
ten years hence when he has made a success or failure of the
Bonniview venture? Head of a trucking firm, oil well driller,
owner of a farm equipment agency? They all cross his mind.
He encourages his employees as well as his children to call
him by his first name, as if he were reluctant to have any
public status. He would probably explain this aversion of
his to a permanent economic or social identity by saying that
he merely wants to be himself. But even that identity re-
fuses to be defined, just as it does to a lesser degree with his
wife Shirley. Ray laughs at her incessant attempts to be someone different—now a peroxide blonde, now a redhead with
a poodle haircut; following diets, mail-order courses in the
"Wisdom of the East," dressing up in slacks and cowboy
boots and then reverting to femininity—never a dull moment when Shirley is trying to develop a new personality.
But at the same time he is not always very sure of himself.
Far more intelligent, far more sensitive than the first American Tinkham, he has inherited none of Nehemiah's tough
integrity and self-assertiveness. It is easy for him to lose himself, as the phrase goes, and to become a totally different
person: at a prize fight, or after two or three drinks, or at
the scene of a bloody accident. "You should have seen your-
self at the movie," Shirley says when they get home; "you

sat there in the dark imitating every single expression Hum-
phrey Bogart made on the screen."

Ray does not know the difference between hypnotism and
amnesia and "getting religion," but he likes to talk about
them; he likes to read in science fiction about brain-washing
and thought control and transmuted identities. "It isn't
scientifically impossible," he says, and he thinks of how he
himself is radically changing the face of the earth on a small
scale. He thinks of the new house, not yet completed, ready
to change its form, its owners, its function at a day's notice.

Bonniview is no more immune to the spiritual forces at
large than were Illium and Jerusha. Ray is no less moved by
an urge to apprehend truth than were Nehemiah and Pliny.
If he has unconsciously destroyed the order which his father
had established, and made his home a very different place,
much freer, in many ways much poorer, it is chiefly because he has wanted to eliminate some of the stages between
reality and himself as his predecessors tried to do. He sees
the relationship in his own characteristic terms: he sees himself not as a child of God wishing to learn the parental command, not as a child of Nature heeding the good impulse,
but as an efficient and reliable instrument for transforming
the invisible power within him into a power adapted to the
world as he knows it.

Several American Landscapes

ONE OF THE benefits which will doubtless come from our increasing concern for the environment is a better understanding of how Americans in the past have felt about the landscape. Each age sees the world in its own manner and has its own notions of beauty; each of them rediscovers the landscape. We ourselves are in the midst of such a rediscovery; what old values are we likely to discard, what are we likely to retain?

No landscape has ever changed so profoundly and so swiftly as ours; not merely within the recent past but from its very beginning. So completely did the Colonial landscape vanish during the nineteenth century that aside from a few monuments nothing remains of it; we are obliged to rely on the descriptions of travellers, on passages in old diaries, on a few random sketches, if we are to visualize it at all. Moreover, the evidence we have is not easy to interpret. It reveals the unfamiliar picture of a crude environment, small in scale, and discontinuous. Brissot de Warville,* who travelled from Boston to New York by way of Springfield in the 1780's, estimated that less than one third of the land in Massachusetts had been cleared of its original forest cover; he commented on the dense woods and their trees of "prodigious height and girth." New houses, some of them of log, rose in the widely separated clearings, with "fields covered

[From a lecture at the University of Massachusetts, Autumn 1965]
*New Travels in the United States of America, 1788, trans. Mara Soceanu Vamos and Durand Echeverria, ed. Durand Echeverria (Cambridge: The Belknap Press of Harvard University Press, 1964), pp. 107–126.

with stumps left to time to destroy, hiding among the stalks
of Indian corn." He noted the enormous heaps of half-rotten
trees blown down by the wind, the fences made of stumps—
roots and all—or of whole trees, along the road near Springfield. The road itself was little more than a wide rough path,
zig-zagging among the stumps and rocks and puddles. There
in the heart of New England was still a pioneer landscape.

Had he travelled in the older, more densely settled areas
along the coast or near the cities he would have been no less
astonished. He would have been struck by the absence of
trees instead of by their profusion. The anonymous author
of *American Husbandry* who explored the Colonies at the
time of the Revolution remarked that "timber . . . grows so
scarce upon the south coast [of New England] that even fire-
wood in some parts is not cheap and is forced to be brought
down from Maine. They not only cut down timber to
raise their buildings and fences," he added, "but in clearing
the grounds for cultivation they destroy all that comes in
their way as if they had nothing to do but to get rid of it
at all events, as fast as possible."*

As for the farms which occupied the land thus cleared,
they seemed to have been far from models of neatness or
efficiency. "Worse ploughing," said the same writer, "is
nowhere to be seen."† He was critical of other things: "nor
are their instruments well made, or even calculated for the
work they are designed to perform."‡ The fences were usually in such poor repair (except around the houses) that children were set to mind the cattle and keep them out of the

---

American Husbandry, ed. Harry J. Carman, Columbia University
Studies in the History of American Agriculture, No. 6 (New York:
Columbia University Press, 1936), p. 61.
† Ibid., p. 59.   ‡ Ibid., p. 60.

fields of corn and wheat. A good half century earlier Jared
Eliot, the first American to write on agriculture, had warned
farmers to rotate their crops and apply manure instead of
cultivating a field for a year or two and then abandoning it.
He was not heeded; a kind of impatient insensitivity toward
the environment appears to have been characteristic of Colonial America; an urgency to be doing something more congenial. Erosion was common from New Jersey all the way to
South Carolina. Everywhere but among the Pennsylvania
Dutch, yields were mediocre after the first. "Most of the
farmers in this country are, in whatever concerns cattle, the
most negligent, ignorant set of men in the world. Nor do I
know of any country in which animals are worse treated." *

Such was the aspect of much of the American countryside
two hundred years ago. The villages and smaller towns were
scarcely more attractive. The house painted white with dark
green or black shutters, that we persist in identifying with
Colonial New England, did not exist before the 1790's; previous to then it was the custom to stain houses green or red,
or to allow them to weather to a pale gray. The common or
green in the center of the community was all too often a
bleak, uncared-for open space where cows and horses grazed,
children played, and where the militia drilled once or twice
a year. The church, on the other hand, was likely to be imposing, and the local inn or tavern was almost always comfortable. No doubt there were shade trees in the yards of
many villagers and farmers; the wineglass elm, to us a symbol of New England, grew as a volunteer in the fields and
along the fences. The tree-lined village street, like the tree-
lined country road, did not become a familiar feature until

* Ibid., p. 59.

the turn of the century. What ornamental planting there was
—and there was a little of it—served an architectural purpose. When the Lombardy poplar was first introduced in
the 1780's it at once became fashionable. It was planted in
rows in front of public buildings, around commons, and even
in cemeteries. Jefferson hoped to have poplars line every
avenue in the new Federal City. An Englishman travelling
in Massachusetts after the Revolution complained that
farmers were everywhere planting Lombardy poplars to
replace the elms they had cut down. Its popularity derived
not from any love of greenery but from its urban formality.
The taste lasted a good thirty years; a sign that it was out
of date was the decision of the mayor of Boston in 1837 to
cut down all the poplars in the Common.

The smooth, close-cropped lawn was unheard of. Perhaps
there was an orchard or a vegetable garden at the rear of
the house, and in front, well protected against wandering
livestock by a fence, a bed of herbs or of flowers. Yet even
this modest display was unusual; Priestley, among other
foreigners, expressed his dismay at the neglected appearance
of most American country dwellings; only the well to do had
flourishing gardens.

It is from such fragments that we are forced to recon-
struct the landscape of an earlier America. The picture,
though far from complete, does not suggest the kind of rural
environment we in the twentieth century are likely to choose.
No doubt the background of forested hills and clear rivers,
the proximity of the wilderness and of the lonely seacoast
with its marshes—all in their pristine freshness—compen-
sated for much. Yet the clearings littered with decaying trees,
the gaunt, shadeless villages, the muddy roads, the abandoned fields with fences in disrepair—these are certainly not

the accepted ingredients of landscape beauty. Nevertheless, it is clear not only that the inhabitants thought their country pleasant and inviting but that many foreigners enjoyed traveling through it.

How are we to account for this? Perhaps by noting those features which foreigners thought worthy of praise. They disliked our roads, the absence of bridges, the discomfort of all public conveyances. The natural scenery, when they noted it at all, was approved. But what most of them admired were the indications of a new and freer kind of society. They liked the comfortable farmhouses for all their absence of paint; they liked the farms which belonged to the small farmers; they even liked the villages, where citizens gathered together to make their own laws. Even the backwoods scenery of stumps and fallen trees was admirable because it suggested a life of independence and resourcefulness. The towns and cities offered even more: the new hospital or prison conducted according to "philanthropic" principles, the society for the emancipation of slaves or for the encouragement of industry. But even the smallest hamlet, the most remote farm, was seen as a sort of social institution. All else was temporary background, scarcely worth noting. "In Italy," Crevecoeur wrote, "all the objects of contemplation, all the the reveries of a traveller, must have reference to ancient generations and to very distant periods. . . . Here, on the contrary, everything is modern, peaceful and benign. . . . Here everything would inspire the reflecting traveler with the most philanthropic ideas. . . . Here he might contemplate the very beginnings and outlines of human society." *

The American landscape was beautiful because it reflected

* *Letters from an American Farmer* (London and Toronto: J. M. Dent and Sons, Ltd.; New York: E. P. Dutton and Co., 1912), p. 11.

a social order which was free and egalitarian. Its beauty was
that of a symbol which men united in venerating. This remains true, whether we always acknowledge it or not, of
many other examples of landscape beauty. But what happens
when we are concerned with other aspects of the environment? Does the verdict necessarily change? Or do we still
find beauty in the landscape because after all it belongs to
us?

The development of a feeling for natural beauty is a familiar aspect of the Romantic movement. It had its prophets
among American writers and painters, and its disciples among
tourists and part-time explorers. Here it was a question
of rediscovering landscapes which had long been known and
inhabited, or of discovering within those landscapes qualities
which had been ignored. The Catskills, the Adirondacks, the
White Mountains were far from being mysterious regions at
the turn of the century, but their wealth of natural beauty
was only apparent to a later generation. The delights afforded
by the spectacle of forest, mountains, lakes, and torrents
in their original state were often intense; they derived in
part from the belief that the landscape untouched by man
revealed most clearly the spirit of its Creator, and that the
solitary spectator could merge his identity with nature, and
be inspired by the experience to a greater self-understanding.
At best the experience was a private affair, not easily described; but on a smaller, less significant scale it could be
repeated; all that was needed was an appropriate setting—a
setting which had some of the qualities of the natural
landscape.

The introduction of the informal or "picturesque" or
natural school of landscape design in America occurred
later than it did in Europe. A few dates will serve to indicate

its growth in popularity. In 1825 André Parmentier, a French nurseryman, designed a "picturesque" garden of some seven acres to display his wares. A number of landowners in New York and the Hudson Valley were soon inspired to produce "picturesque" parks and gardens of their own. In 1831 Mt. Auburn Cemetery in Cambridge, Massachusetts, became the first large-scale example of "picturesque" landscaping in America. It, too, was soon imitated in most of the Eastern cities, and it aroused wide interest in the recreational possibilities of a less formal kind of park. In 1841, Andrew Jackson Downing, the first professional landscape architect in the country, published his book on landscape gardening* which gave practical suggestions as to how the new style could be adapted to American conditions. In 1853 Llewellyn Park in New Jersey became the first community to be laid out in the "picturesque" style, and finally in 1856 Olmsted and Vaux won the competition for the design of Central Park with their large-scale "picturesque" composition. By that time the prestige of the style was firmly established.

A revolution in ways of perceiving and enjoying the environment, if it is serious, has to be more than a few influential books and innovative designs. It has to operate through ten thousand private decisions, and those in turn have to be triggered in countless different ways: by reading a poem or seeing a picture; by wishing to repeat a memorable experience or to astonish a neighbor; by dissatisfaction, by sudden illumination, by patient experimentation. The new Romantic feel for the natural environment and the desire to reproduce

A Treatise on the Theory and Practice of Landscape Gardening Adapted to North America, with a View to the Improvement of Country Residences: With Remarks on Rural Architecture (New York and London: Wiley and Putnam, 1841).

it expressed itself simultaneously all over America. A house was painted brown instead of white; a holiday was passed in tramping through the woods; a milldam was suddenly seen as a desecration; a law was passed to protect songbirds. Trees were planted along the village street; in 1853 the first village improvement association was founded in Stockbridge, Massachusetts. "Improvement" meant beautifying the common and the cemetery and the roads leading into town. Philanthropy in the Colonial sense of the word played no part in the concept. The example spread rapidly, and one village after another undertook to adorn its streets, its parks, its cemeteries, the campus of the local college or seminary with greenery. Much of the small-town East and South still shows the results of this labor of love, and gradually the stark landscape surviving from the eighteenth century was transformed. It was Downing who first launched the crusade by holding up to scorn the villages "of old wooden houses out of repair . . . new wooden houses distressingly lean in their proportions, chalky white in their clapboards, and *spinachy* green in their blinds. The church is absolutely hideous—a long box of cardboard with a huge pepper box on top. There is not a tree in the streets."* Even the once esteemed Greek Revival façade was condemned along with the Lombardy poplar, the gridiron pattern of streets, and the symmetrical flower garden.

Does it matter that this taste for the "picturesque" in architecture and gardening was largely confined to a sophisticated and prosperous middle class? Its impact on the less worldly Midwest and on the growing manufacturing towns

* "On the Improvement of Country Villages," in *Downing's Rural Essays*, ed. George William Curtis (New York: George A. Leavitt, 1869), p. 229.

was slight. But if the designed environment was of necessity
limited to a group which could afford to remodel its houses
and grounds, the philosophy back of the movement affected
almost every American by causing him to see his environment in a different way. A beautiful landscape came to mean
a natural landscape, one which man had altered little or not
at all. Contact, however brief, with such a landscape led to
an awareness of eternal values and to a questioning of one's
ultimate identity. In this the American version of Romanticism differed not at all from the Romanticism of Europe;
there was nothing at first glance to distinguish the effect of
the American landscape on the beholder from the effect
of the Alps or the Scottish Highlands. Nevertheless, there
began to evolve—without ever achieving a coherent form—a
belief that American landscape beauty was unlike any other,
and that it was producing a unique American character. An
anonymous writer in an art magazine in 1853* attempted
to find the answer to a twofold question: What was American scenery, and how did it influence the character of Americans? After enumerating some of more spectacular Eastern
sights—the Great Lakes, the Falls of the Potomac, the Adirondacks, the Hudson Valley—the author concluded that
this scenery must inevitably affect the spirit of the people
who lived in the midst of it. He cited the parallel between
the clarity and grandeur of Greek scenery and the clarity
and grandeur of Greek art; but for America he could find no
instance. Perhaps the future would produce it. For he was
convinced that the landscape of America revealed the intent
of the Creator to form an American identity. "The Infinite
is influencing us in natural scenery, and in the presence of

---

* "American Scenery," *International Magazine of Art* (New York,
1853).

mountains and lakes and rivers, lending, through the sense of the infinite, something of His own grandeur of soul."

In its small way the "picturesque" garden or park, the holiday glimpse of the forest offered the same inspiration; they were substitutes for the wider natural landscape from which we as Americans were deriving our nationality. Once again beauty in the landscape was a symbol; not of an enlightened social order as it had been a century before, but of a divine purpose for America.

The revolutionary phase of the Romantic approach to the environment was over by the time of the Civil War, but it can be said (and often *is* said) with some justification that the essential philosophy of Romanticism still determines our attitude toward the landscape and still inspires our designs. We still try to preserve areas of natural beauty and try to reproduce its qualities in our man-made environments —and for a reason much the same as that of our nineteenth-century predecessors: we wish to be reminded that we are (in the old-fashioned phrase) "part of nature." Certainly there has been no explicit repudiation of the Romantic approach among landscape architects or conservationists or the growing numbers of Americans worried about the environment.

All the old loyalties are reaffirmed, the old phrases used, but do they really mean the same in 1969 as they did in 1869? It was, in fact, after the Civil War that signs of a distinct change in our attitude toward the natural environment began to multiply. They originated significantly enough among those who were concerned with the condition of our cities, specifically with conditions in the slums. Here was an environment which was the opposite of natural or inspiring. Crime and disease proliferated in narrow streets and in crowded and filthy tenements. As the philosophy of the times understood it, the solution was to bring in light and air and space. The architect could not solve the problem by himself; the whole city was involved.

It is scarcely necessary to say that the mid-nineteenth-century attempt to purify and reform the city did not succeed. But it eventually led to a more prosaic definition of environmental influences and to an attempt to control them chiefly for the benefit of men's health. Nature as a manifestation of the Infinite became nature as a resource, and this resource was broken down into its component parts, each being examined for its usefulness. The forest became the storehouse of water, the modifier of climates; the park became in common parlance the lungs of the city. Sunlight killed germs, trees cooled the high temperature of the streets, and so did lakes and rivers. Privacy prevented the rapid spread of disease, and space was where children acquired bodily vigor and resistance to infection. The American city undertook to build its own simulated natural environment.

What the city reformers did or tried to do was done according to their field by foresters, agronomists, soil experts, conservationists, engineers, and eventually all the environmental design professions: nature was reinterpreted as a resource to be efficiently managed and controlled. But in the long run it was the city which determined attitudes toward the natural environment, not the farmer or the woodsman or the hunter. It is because of the city that we have learned to think of nature as a process; it is because of the city and its needs that we are determined to have this process continue without interruption or diminution. The current enthusiasm for ecology is urban-minded, through and through. The natural area is to be protected not only because it con-

serves water (for industrial or municipal use), purifies the
air (of urban wastes), muffles traffic noises, increases real
estate value, and provides scientists with a laboratory, but
because it offers an inexpensive and effective psychotherapy
for weary urban holiday makers. No one will question the
importance of those benefits; indeed, there is increasing
evidence that we will demand them in every part of the
country, for every population. But as we continue to require
of the natural landscape that it perform certain essential
services, it is logical that we judge the value of that landscape by its performance. What we even now call a beautiful landscape may not necessarily be efficient, but certainly
in the future an efficient landscape, a landscape where the
health-giving processes are continuous and unimpeded, will
be thought of as beautiful.

Other-directed Houses

WRITING IN *Harper's Magazine* almost for the last time before his death, Bernard De Voto expressed himself on a subject close to the heart of many Americans: the increasing untidiness and ugliness of much of the landscape. He described what had happened to the New England countryside as a result of the invasion of tourists and vacation-seekers, and was incensed by the roadside developments in places which a few years ago had still been unspoiled. U.S. Highway 1 in Maine came in for harsh words: "As far as Bucksport it has become what it has been from Newburyport on: a longitudinal slum. It is an intermittent eyesore of drive-ins, diners, souvenir stands, purulent amusement parks, cheapjack restaurants and the kind of cabins my companion describes as mailboxes."*

Mr. De Voto's sentiments are impeccable and have been applauded and echoed by many thousands who travel the country by car either for business or pleasure, by planning and landscape experts, civic improvement groups, highway engineers, and by foreigners now seeing America for the first time. And this mounting public indignation, together with the Federal Highway Program, clearly suggests that we have reached the point of attempting some sort of reform in the treatment of our highway margins.

U.S. Highway 1 is in fact one of the most sensationally ugly roads in America, and there is a particular stretch of it, somewhere between Washington and Baltimore, which when photographed through a telescopic lens seems to epit-

[From *Landscape*, Vol. 6, No. 2, Winter 1956–57]
* "The Easy Chair," *Harper's Magazine* (October 1955), p. 12.

omize the degradation which in the last few years has over-
whelmed our highways. Two sluggish streams of traffic, cars
bumper to bumper, move as best they can over a hopelessly
inadequate roadbed between jungles of billboards and roadside stands, each sprouting a dozen signs of its own, and
each with its own swarm of parked cars in front. This ex-
tends out of sight for miles and miles, varied here and there
by a set of traffic lights.

To a lesser degree these conditions exist intermittently
throughout the heavily populated East and Midwest. Even
in the West things can be pretty bad near any large city or
along any heavily traveled highway. But by and large congestion is not a prime problem in the greater part of the
country; it is the phenomenal growth of roadside establishments that most of America has to worry about. The West
is tourist country, which means that roadside businesses have
their own special public, a generous and numerous one in
the summer season; but at the same time the region is slowly
becoming self-conscious about its man-made appearance
and is wondering what it can do to control its highway margins. Most likely there are highway stretches there as hideous
as anywhere in the United States. Highway 66, for instance,
which traverses some of the finest scenery in New Mexico
and Arizona, would be a disgrace (as far as mutilation of the
landscape is concerned) to the Jersey Meadows. Its horrors
end by fascinating the traveler so that he pays little or no
attention to the wider view; but there are plenty of tourists
who try to find an alternate route.

It would be hard (though not impossible) to exaggerate
the extent of this blight. But still we must give these roadside establishments their due. They are entitled to their day
in court, and so far they have not had it. Many have experi-

enced driving for hour after hour across an emptiness—desert
or prairie—which was *not* blemished by highway stands.
How relieved and delighted one always is to finally see somewhere in the distance the jumble of billboards and gas pumps
and jerry-built houses. Tourist traps or not, these are very
welcome sights, and even the commands to EAT, COME AS
YOU ARE, GAS UP, GET FREE ICE WATER AND STICKERS, have
a comforting effect. Common report has it that these people
get as much of your money as they can. Rarely is this the
case; they usually have a friendliness and a willingness to
help which somehow comes with their job. The gaudier
the layout the nicer it seems, and its impact on the surrounding landscape bothers not at all.

Another kind of encounter with Mr. De Voto's longitudinal slums is found when flying. Somewhere (over western
Kansas, perhaps) it begins to grow dark and at first all one
can see is a dark mottled brown world under an immaculate
sky of deep blue steel; then one flies over some small rec-
tangular pattern of scattered lights—a farm town—and out
of it, like the tail of a comet, stretches a long sinuous line of
lights of every color and intensity, a stream of concentrated
multicolored brilliance, some of it moving, some of it wink-
ing and sparkling, and every infinitesimal point of color distinct in the clear night air. The stream pours itself into the
black farmlands, into the prairie, and vanishes. This of
course is the roadside development seen from an altitude of
several thousand feet; the most beautiful and in a way the
most moving spectacle the western flight can offer, because
for the first time you see that man's work can be an adorn-
ment to the face of the earth.

Fleeting beauty, then, and occasional usefulness; how
much more can be said of many other of our products?

When high-minded groups vie with each other in bitter condemnation of the highway developments, devising legal and
moral means of destroying them, those two glimpses come
to mind. Would it not be better—fairer, that is to say, and
more intelligent—to see if the potentialities of these roadside slums cannot somehow be realized for the greater profit
and pleasure of all.

A liking for this feature of the human landscape of A-
merica should not blind anyone to its frequent depravity and
confusion and dirt. Its potentialities for trouble—aesthetic,
social, economic—are as great as its potentialities for good,
and indeed it is this ambidexterity which gives the highway
and its margins so much significance and fascination. But
how are we to tame this force unless we understand it and
even develop a kind of love for it? We have not really tried
to understand it as yet. For one thing we know little or
nothing about how the roadside development, the strip,
came into being, nor about how it grows. We know (and
seem to care) far too little about the variety of businesses
which comprise it. Why is it that certain enterprises proliferate in certain areas and not in others, why are some of them
clustered together, and others are far apart? Which of
them are dependent on the nearby town and city, which
of them depend on transients? The modern highway is of
course the origin and sustainer of them all, but what a
complex thing the modern highway has become; how varied
its functions and how varied the public which makes use
of it! To the factory or warehouse on its margin it is essentially the equivalent of the railroad; to the garage or service
station it means direct accessibility to the passing public.
The local businessman thinks of it as a way to reach and
exploit the outlying suburban and rural areas, the farmer

thinks of it as a way to reach town; the tourist thinks of
it as an amenity, and the transcontinental bus or trucking
company thinks of it as the shortest distance between two
widely separated points. Each of these interests not only
has its own idea of how the highway is to be designed and
traced; it brings its own special highway service establishments into being. Which of the lot are we to eliminate?

Or perhaps it is more a question of which of them we are
to save, for more than one program of highway reform calls
for the almost complete suppression of them all. If asked to
make a distinction among them with a view to finding out
which were to survive and in what proportion, one could say
that they roughly fell into two classes: those establishments
serving the working economy, and those serving our leisure.

In the first would naturally fall all the factories, warehouses, truck depots, service stations, used car lots, shopping
centers and so on—the rollcall is endless; and in the second
would be restaurants, cafes, night-clubs, amusement parks,
drive-in movies, souvenir stands, motels—for motels are
primarily associated with vacation travel and with leisure;
in brief all those enterprises which Mr. De Voto listed and
denounced, and then some. What is more, these two classes—
the workaday and the leisure—should be of almost equal
value, though kept well apart, at least when we were consider-
ing which businesses would be allowed along the highway
outside of built-up areas.

A reason for so doing can be easily given: one of the
unique aspects of the modern American highway (an aspect
often overlooked) is that it has now become the place where
we spend more and more of our leisure. It plays the role
which Main Street or the Park or the Courthouse Square
used to play in the free time of our pedestrian predecessors:

the place where we go to enjoy ourselves and spend our leisure hours. Never was the lure of the open road so powerful, so irresistible as now; for merely to *be* on a highway, entirely without a destination in view, is to many of every class and age a source of unending pleasure. Is this an exaggeration? Eliminate from any stretch of highway—always outside the largest cities and the great industrial areas—the motorists who are driving purely for enjoyment, either on vacation or for a breath of fresh air or to show off the new car or in search of a good time, and you would eliminate more than a third of the normal traffic. This mass movement onto the highways is in no manner mysterious: given more and more leisure—not merely in terms of holidays and vacations but shorter daily working hours—and given more and more cars, what is the inevitable result? The highways leading out of our towns and cities are alive with cars, driving when work is over and before the evening meal to see how the new subdivision is getting on; out to the Dairy Queen five miles east to have a giant malt; to the drive-in movie still further away; cars with couples necking, souped-up cars racing down the measured mile; cars playing chicken, cars, pickups, motorcycles, scooters all driving merely for the sake of driving. "Gliding up and down for no purpose that I could see—not to eat, not for love, but only gliding." And this leisure traffic is multiplied many times over on Sundays and holidays. Foolish or not, dangerous, unprofitable, unhealthy or otherwise, these are the ways we spend many of our carefree hours, and the highway is an essential adjunct of them all. Thus any highway reform program which has at the back of its mind the old-fashioned notion that our roads are really nothing but means for fast and efficient long distance transportation, to the neglect of the leisurely pleasure seeker and the establishments which exist to serve him, will run head on into a flourishing American institution. It may well be that the collision will end in the defeat of the reformers.

The need to recognize and understand the importance of that portion of the longitudinal slum associated with our free-time motorized activities must not be overlooked. It is very likely that the present mood of highway reform will expend itself chiefly on those establishments least organized, least equipped economically to protect themselves, and this highway development (or more accurately speaking, this whole aspect of American life) holds enormous promise of future growth, aesthetic as well as social. This promise is not always very evident. Our highways margins are littered not only with the decaying refuse of what might be called the premotorized-leisure age—shanties, one-pump filling stations, rows of empty overnight cabins, miserable bars— they are also growing a second jungle crop of ill-planned, ill-designed, uneconomic enterprises. These still far outnumber the good ones. One American town and city after another is finding to its shame that its highway approaches are becoming intolerably ugly and unwholesome. And the aftermath of this discovery is more often than not a wholesale condemnation, especially on the part of the right-thinking, of the local highway strip.

We have become entirely too fastidious, too conformist, in architectural matters. In our recently acquired awareness of architectural values we have somehow lost sight of the fact that there is still such a thing as a popular taste in art quite distinct from the educated taste, and that popular taste often evolves in its own way. Not that a recognition of such a distinction would automatically lead to an acceptance of roadside architecture; most of it, by any standards, is bad. But it would perhaps allow us to see that highway architecture is changing and improving very rapidly all around us, and allow us to find certain virtues—or at least certain qualities—in it worth respecting and fostering. In all those streamlined façades, in all those flamboyant entrances and deliberately bizarre decorative effects, those cheerfully self-assertive masses of color and light and movement that clash so roughly with the old and traditional, there are certain underlying characteristics which suggest that we are confronted not by a debased and cheapened art, but a kind of folk art in mid-twentieth-century garb.

We must accustom ourselves to the fact that the basic motive in the design of these establishments—whether motels or drive-in movies or nightclubs—is a desire to please and attract the passerby. The austere ambitions of the contemporary architect to create a self-justifying work of art have no place in this other part of town. Here every business has to woo the public—a public, moreover, which passes by at forty miles or more an hour—if it is to survive. The result is an *other-directed architecture*, and the only possible criterion of its success is whether or not it is liked; the consumer, not the artist or the critic, is the final court of appeal.

This to be sure is true of almost every retail business: they all have eye appeal. But a downtown business catering to pedestrians can concentrate on relatively modest display, whereas a highway leisure time enterprise not only has to catch the eye of the motorist, it has to offer a special attraction of its own: it has to suggest pleasure and good times. This is not always easy to do: an appearance of hospitality or inexpensiveness or reliability is not enough. What there has to be is the absence of any hint of the workaday world which presumably is being left behind: any hint of the domestic, the institutional, the severely practical, the economical; any hint of the common or plain. On the contrary, what is essential, both inside and out, is an atmosphere of luxury, gaiety, of the unusual and unreal. Imitation is quite as good as the genuine thing if the effect is convincing and the customer is happy. Go into a roadside dine-and-dance in a non-holiday mood (as happens when you stop to make a phone call) and you are affronted by the shoddy decorations, the crude indirect lighting, the menu, and the music. But go in when you are looking for a good time and for an escape from the everyday, and at once the place seems steeped in magic. It is a glimpse of another world.

The effectiveness of this architecture is finally a matter of what that other world is: whether it is one that you have been dreaming about or not. And it is here that you begin to discover the real vitality of this new other-directed architecture along our highways: it is creating a dream environment for our leisure that is totally unlike the dream environment of a generation ago. It is creating and at the same time reflecting a new public taste.

Most of us can recall a time when our leisure and holiday activities were essentially imitations of the everyday activities of a superior social group—the so-called leisure class. If we dressed up on formal occasions it was because these enviable people dressed that way all the time, and our dress was an imitation of theirs. We went to hotels which resembled at a dozen removes the palace of a prince, to movie houses which resembled court operas, to restaurants and bars a-dorned with mahogany and crystal and gold. All places associated with group good times—football stadiums, circuses, theaters, transatlantic steamers, even stations and parlor cars, were designed and decorated to suggest a way of life more sumptuous than our own. Such was the other-directed architecture of the period: in the Victorian phrase, our good times were largely spent in aping our betters.

It is hard to say when this class imitation lost its appeal. Undoubtedly the Depression, by reducing the number and wealth of the leisure class as well as its prestige, had much to do with it. Still, its architectural manifestations lasted until the end of World War Two. The older and more traditional regions of the country continued until a few years ago (although with decreasing enthusiasm) to design many of its places of public entertainment to look Colonial or Olde Englishe—for the antique also had its snob appeal. What actually speeded the revolution in taste was something quite outside the field of art: it was the fact that the wage-earning class began to acquire more leisure than the executive or professional class had, and began to have more money than before. It was at last in a position to set its own pace in leisure activities and attitudes.

And if we bear in mind that along with this increased leisure came a renewed flood of automobiles, we should have no trouble in understanding what happened: the new leisure ideal became a hankering after what advertising copy writers call "vacationland." We wanted to spend our free time not in a superior social world but in a world remote in terms of space. Yet vacationland is still only attainable once or twice a year; for the rest of the time we have to find a substitute, and it was in response to that need that every place of popular entertainment, and in particular every roadside place, rose up and transformed itself. At once the white tablecloth, the waiter in dinner jacket, the potted palm, the Louis xvi decorations were banished. Names like Astor and Ritz and

Ambassador dropped out of the popular world to be replaced
by Casa Mañana, Bali, Sirocco, Shangri-La. The new drive-
in movies built along every highway and outside every town
ignored the old prestige names of Rivoli and Criterion and
Excelsior to call themselves The Lariat, the Rocket, the
Cornhusker. Motels designed to look like New England villages or California Missions or Southern plantations (depending on their location) were all but crowded out of business by brand-new establishments inspired by Futurama,
Hawaii, Hollywood, the Caribbean. Swimming pools and
exotic planting made them even more inviting.

A sudden increase in holiday and freetime travel, faster
and more comfortable cars, more money to spend, all helped
precipitate the change. Across the country at strategic intervals of one hundred to one hundred and fifty miles (the
average distance covered between meals) one new and expensive highway strip after another burst into activity. Sometimes they rose outside of large cities, more often they rose
next to some small town remote from any neighbor. In every
case their presence affected the local pattern of leisure activities even while it served the traveling public. Never before had there been so total and dramatic a transformation
of a portion of the American landscape, so sudden an evolution in habits, nor such a flowering of popular architecture.

Is it necessary to add that along with this development
came a rash of billboards and a totally unrelated growth of
highway-based industries? That chaos overtook countless
communities and that much of the old landscape was damaged
beyond repair? Those are the features we are not allowed to
forget, the ones we lament. But they cannot entirely hide
from us the fact that a new kind of architecture, popular

in the truest sense, was for the first time given an opportunity
to evolve.

Well, it has not yet finished its evolution by any means,
but some of its more salient characteristics are already becoming evident. At the moment flashiness seems to be the
chief of these: a flashiness of color and design that over-
shoots its mark. In time we will learn how to astonish and
attract, how to suggest exotic vacationland without re-
sorting to shock treatment. Walls canted out for no good
reason, façades placed at an angle to the highway and over-
dramatized (while the other sides are left in their native
cement-block nakedness), these are more or less clumsy at-
temps to capture the passerby's attention, something which
could be done by other means.

Actually the style already possesses two other characteristics ideally suited to this purpose, its use of lights and its
use of signs. Neon lights, floodlights, fluorescent lights, spot-
lights, moving and changing lights of every strength and color
—these constitute one of the most original and potentially
creative elements in the other-directed style. It would be
hard to find a better formula for obliterating the workaday
world and substituting that of the holiday than this: night-
time and a garden of moving colored lights. It is perhaps too
much to say that the neon light is one of the great artistic
innovations of our age, but one wonders what a Gothic or a
Baroque architect would have done to exploit its theatrical
and illusionist possibilities, its capacity to transform not
only a building but its immediate environment. The contemporary architect will have none of it, and while he makes
much of his synthesizing of all arts, the ones he chooses
are usually the traditional fresco and mural and mosaic.
Matisse and Dufy might have designed in neon with great

success, and so for that matter could any imaginative sculptor. A prejudice against any taint of commercialism in decoration is so strong in a segment of the public that one of the chief targets of civic reform groups is usually the local display of neon lights. And yet one would have to be blind indeed not to respond to the fantastic beauty of any neon lighted strip after dark.

The second basic characteristic of the other-directed architecture is the liberal use of signs. Their purpose is obvious: to indentify and promote the business. But they also serve to help establish the mood at hand, and even to complete the artistic composition. The tendency seems to be for all signs connected with roadside establishments to grow larger, more conspicuous and more elaborate. One reason for this is well explained by Mobilgas in a bulletin telling its dealers why the Mobil sign outside service stations is to be changed: "Today's motorist drives fifty or sixty miles an hour in the open country. He is often miles from home and doesn't know where the next Mobil service station is. So he must have plenty of advance notice. . . . The problem of long range visibility becomes extremely important. . . . The old Mobilgas shield was designed to go with Colonial type service stations which once dotted New England and New York. But as the company expanded its marketing area and functional streamlined stations replaced the Colonial design, the shield took on a somewhat out-of-date and out-of-place appearance."

The new sign, fittingly enough, is the work of an industrial designer formerly connected with Futurama.

But aside from this very practical reason the signs are large because they are held to be ornamental. Great pylons, masts, walls thrusting out toward the passerby serve very

often to balance the architectural composition and are part
of its fantastic and unreal charm. And since modesty has
no place along the highway, there seems to be nothing to
prevent an even further increase in size. Eventually, let us
hope, the sign will concentrate in itself most of the distant
eye appeal, and allow the building to assume a more restful
and conventional appearance.

These, then, are some of the peculiarities of the new
architecture lining our highways and catering to our leisure
hours: conspicuous façades, exotic decoration and landscaping,
a lavish use of lights and colors and signs, and an indiscriminate borrowing and imitating to produce certain pleasing
effects. They are by no means the ingredients of a serious
or lasting style, but the idiom is still only about ten years
old. At present it already manages on occasion to achieve
very attractive and gay effects ideally suited to its festive
purpose.

The trouble is these successes are few and far between.
They often suffer moreover from being located in the midst
of confusion. One remedy for this (and also a partial remedy
for the whole condition of the highway margin) would be
the elimination of billboards. They serve no constructive
purpose, they are unsightly, and they blight their immediate
surroundings; no one likes them and they have many powerful enemies; if they were to go, the highway jungle would
be reduced to manageable proportions and many unsuspected
architectural and urbanist qualities would for the first time
become visible. However we should allow local firms and
services to advertise. Their signs often provide information
not to be found elsewhere and which the stranger approaching a town has to have; and here again it must be pointed
out that limitations on size are increasingly unrealistic.

Even state highway departments are awakening to the fact
that a public traveling at sixty miles an hour cannot be
served by signs designed to be read at half that speed.

With some justice we complain of the shoddy construction and poor design of our highway establishments, the
total lack of any comprehensive scheme or of any harmony
between the several parts of a strip development. But the
wonder is that they are as good as they frequently are. Is
there any architectural school in the country which ac-
knowledges the existence and the importance of a popular,
other-directed architecture meant for pleasure and popular
mass entertainment? We have forgotten, it seems, that architecture can sometimes smile and be light-hearted, and
that leisure, no less than study or work, calls for an appropriate setting. Yet the few roadside establishments designed by
imaginative and skillful architects are so immensely superior
to the rest that they have almost at once been imitated. At
present the average highway resort—motel, drive-in movie,
restaurant or nightclub—has been put up by the owner
with no sort of guidance but his own limited experience and
taste; at best by a building contractor. The display signs are
usually the product of an industrial firm knowing nothing of
the location or the public. The lighting itself is the work of
the local electrician, relying on catalogs for inspiration. The
landscaping is done by the local nurseryman, and the planning, the location, the relationship to the neighbors and to the
highway is little more than an adjustment to local zoning
restrictions or to the edicts of the highway department. We
need not be astonished at the results.

Both of these hallmarks of an other-directed architecture
—lighting and display—cry out for intelligent and artistic
handling. In these fields we could learn much from Europe,

for architects and decorators abroad have not been handicapped by the notion that the architect should have nothing
to do with the promotional phases of his project. In Europe
neon lighting often betrays a feeling for color and design
and mood. A rollerskating rink demands different treatment,
different colors, than a restaurant or a motel; yet we see
many of all three trimmed in the same bright green and
harsh red. We also suffer in this country from that malady
which Victor Hugo, a little-appreciated writer on architecture, said had killed architecture in the Western World:
the tyranny of the printed word. The printed (or painted
or illuminated) word has not killed architecture in America
or anywhere else, but it threatens at times to overpower it,
to thwart it. Our neon lights, capable of expressing a genuine
poetry, have so far only been taught to shout PEPSICOLA,
CAFE, STOP, and the tyranny of the word in other forms, its
poverty and monotony, is nowhere more in evidence than in
the clutter of letters outside every town and city, when a
few universally recognized symbols would suffice to communicate the same messages more rapidly and with less fa-
tigue to the eye. Once more the European highway signs are
clearer and neater and better understood than our own inscriptions—not to mention those traditional trade emblems—
the barber's dish, the tobacconist's cigar, the butcher's flag,
the locksmith's key, which enliven the European street without destroying its unity. Here is where the advertising expert could well do us a valuable service: by devising a set
of symbols for roadside use to replace the present nightmare
of words.

Has the planner no contribution to make? Is it not possible to introduce order and harmony even in the midst of a
collection of heterogeneous enterprises? Shopping centers

show us something which we would not have believed possible a decade or more ago: that diverse businesses can willingly come together in one location, subject themselves to certain controls, learn to think in terms of a small community, and still prosper as never before. Their location off the highway with their own ample parking space likewise makes them models for other groupings. Most highway pleasure spots are hopelessly scattered; some wedged in between truck depots and service stations, others far out among the empty lots. They belong in each other's company; they are meant to share the same atmosphere of good times. If they were grouped together in clusters of, say, six at frequent intervals, traffic confusion would be reduced, and the establishments themselves would be protected. Some of them appear to belong logically together: restaurants, drive-in movies, motels and souvenir stands; and for a different (and perhaps a younger) public: sports arenas, drive-in refreshment stands, and dance halls.

For any such systematic and orderly strip development a new kind of zone, a "Zone of Amusements," would have to be recognized and created, and then protected from intrusion on the part of workaday businesses or residences. It is in the organizing and rehabilitating of this neglected and misunderstood part of the community that the planner and architect and industrial designer and advertising expert could work together.

Will they have the chance to do it? Let us hope that the merits and charm of the highway strip are not so obscure but that they will be accepted by the wider public; that our professed and frequently genuine regard for the small business will protect these smallest of small businessmen from extinction, and in some manner give them a firmer footing in the community. And let us hope that all those architectural and planning skills, the advertiser's knowledge of public taste and custom would welcome the opportunity to broaden their scope and to work together. We can be sure of none of these things. A tide of urban improvement is beginning to rise all over the country, and it is reinforced by public money and a kind of impatience with nonconformity, as noticeable on the left as on the right. What local zeal cannot achieve may well be achieved by the Federal Highway Program: the sterilizing of our roadsides.

It is finally a question of which force proves the stronger: the demand for an efficient and expensive highway system designed primarily to serve the working economy of the country, or a new and happy concept of leisure with its own economic structure, its own art forms, and its own claim on a share of the highway. At present we are indifferent to this promise for our culture, and to the extinction which threatens it; is it not time that we included this new part of America in our concern? It is true that we can no longer enter our towns and cities on avenues leading among meadows and lawns and trees, and that we often enter them instead through roadside slums. But we can if we choose transform these approaches into avenues of gaiety and brilliance, as beautiful as any in the world; and it is not yet too late.

Life-worship

NOT MANY of the bright hopes which the nineteenth century held for the future have been realized. There is little in common between the world we inhabit and the paradise of rationalism and technology our forebears dreamed of. Yet in one case they had the gift of accurate prophecy: they prophesied that ours would be the Century of the Child.

For if any one sustained purpose can be said to inspire all our efforts to right society and improve the environment, it is our concern for youth: its health and happiness and opportunities for full development. It has often been remarked that we seem to have lost the gift for devising social and economic Utopias. But by way of compensation we have learned not only to design but to create down to the last detail Utopias for childhood—places which are safe and healthy and beautiful. It is true that these are almost entirely suburbs and family type summer resorts, but what other age has done better? Innumerable communities exist, especially here in America, where the child can play on expanses of lawn without fear of being run over, where he has easy contact with nature and a home adjusted to his needs; where there is the best school money can buy, and where he is exposed to no contamination from the adult world of politics and work. It is appropriate that the ruler and protector of these communities should be a child-oriented apolitical figure, the housewife who divides her almost limitless energies between running the Cub Scouts, agitating birth control, and fighting all nonconforming uses of land.

That it is better to have children happy and safe and well,

[From *Landscape*, Vol. 17, No. 3, Spring 1968]

instead of neglected, should go without saying. But even
these good intentions can be carried to excess; other parts
of the environment need care. A child-centered society can
easily become a biologically centered society, a society obsessed with the sanctity of life without bothering as to its
meaning and end. Thoreau's nonsensical boast that he preferred man as part and parcel of nature to man the member
of society is already far too widely accepted. In terms of the
environment and its reforming, the primacy of the child
means that social change takes second place, and that man-
made beauty comes last of all. Intellectually the American
public knows that our environment must incorporate social
justice; we also know that public art is an essential ingre-
dient of our culture; but what finally arouses us to action is
the discovery of a widespread menace to health. If any
prediction can safely be made it is that we will still have
slums, just as evil as now, long after our rivers and beaches
are relatively clean and the air in our cities relatively pure,
because the health and well-being of our children is at stake.

And as this biological awareness becomes more general it
will increase its area of concern to include not merely the
domestic environment but the environment of leisure and
even the environment of work. We can foresee in the not
very distant future an America transformed. Our cities will
be no more splendid than they are now, but they will be
clean and cheerful and safe; the social order will still be
without justice but it will be clean and cheerful and safe.
The landscape will be purged of its terrors and dangers—
the Sierra Club assures us that the mountain wilderness is
really gentle and friendly—but it will be clean and cheerful
and safe. There will be no monuments or ruins to recall a
turbulent past or to suggest the vanity of our hopes, but it

will be a pleasant world, with only the faintest taint of be-
havioral science and chlorine.

What is the role of the environmental designer in this child-
life oriented world? What it has always been. to satisfy the
demands of his patrons as best he can. Whatever his aesthetic or social convictions he has to learn to mobilize the as-
pirations which exist, not those which textbooks tell him
ought to exist. An environmental philosophy largely based
on ecology as the absence of conflict is necessarily indifferent
to art and to social reform. Even so, there have been worse
philosophies than this: national grandeur or the pursuit of
wealth were merely two of them. But the designer must
learn the rules of the game: to advocate decent housing, not
because slums are an indignity but because they are potential centers of infection; to condemn the ravishing of the
countryside, not because this is wasteful of an important
resource but because recreation sites are imperiled. You will
thus please the embattled parents, the conservationists, and
presumably benefit the child.

   Ingenuity in devising justifications will be needed, but
designers in the past have been faced with the same problem
of satisfying their patrons while at the same time remaining
true to their inner convictions. Provided he pays lip service
to the principles of ecology the contemporary environmental
designer is as free as he ever was to create in terms of hu-
manity and his art.

The Imitation of Nature

RIGHT NOW, at this very moment, somewhere in the United States a forum is being held (or a round table or a symposium) on the problems of the "Expanding Metropolis."

Dedicated men are showing one another colored slides, asking sharp questions from the floor, reading one another papers which will eventually appear in book form.

A characteristic of every such forum is the unanimity of point of view of the participants. Not that they necessarily agree on all minor matters; what they agree on is something basic: on a definition of the modern city as a *social institution*. In the words of Le Corbusier, they consider it a tool, an implement of work. He discussed the city in *Urbanisme*,* many years ago, as a product of man's action against nature, as an organism created by man for protection and work. As the popular phrase has it, the city is for people.

The men uniting in this profession of faith come from all walks of life: they are federal, state, and municipal authorities, sociologists, economists, housing experts, and Guggenheim Fellows. The variety of participants is in fact so great that it is hard to see where the line is drawn. Yet it is noticeable that there are certain persons who as a general rule do *not* attend: geographers, especially physical geographers, meteorologists, and representatives of the natural sciences. Publishers come, but poets and novelists and artists, whose business it is to interpret the modern city, do not. Public health officials are there, but no physicians; social anthropologists but no

[From *Landscape*, Vol. 9, No. 1, Autumn 1959]
* Paris: Editions Cres, 1925.

physical anthropologists; neither the psychologist nor the biologist is heard from.

The Dissenting Voices

All these men are presumably interested in the city and its problems; are they by any chance excluded from the discussion? In a sense, yes; they are disturbed and alienated by the definition. They are in accord that the city is a social institution, but they also think of it as a *place*, a distinct environment where certain relationships evolve not only between men and men, but between men and the forces of nature. They might even define the city as a symbiosis: a living together of two dissimilar organisms in a close association which is advantageous to both. To them the city is a dirty or beautiful or unhealthy or crowded or stimulating place where men should (but cannot always) lead full lives on every level; they cannot think of it simply as a kind of abstract cat's cradle of social relationships.

The social-minded urbanist is quick to retort that he has no objection to this other definition which indeed he considers merely an amplification of his own, and he mentions the gracefully written chapter in the forthcoming book on the necessity of visualizing the city as a potentially healthy and beautiful environment with as much sunlight and greenery as possible. He means this; the fact that he thinks of nature in the two-dimensional terms of Le Corbusier should not be held against him. He fights none the less bravely and effectively for green spaces and parks. Just the same, the divergence in points of view between the social minded and what might be called the symbiotic minded is a fundamental one. Properly developed, it is the divergence between an established

orthodoxy which has ceased to question its basic tenets,
and a radically new approach; between those who think of
man exclusively as a social economic being and those who
think of him in broader terms.

Man Belongs to Nature

The symbiotic approach to the problem of the city has an
extremely simple and familiar premise. It is that man, in
addition to his spiritual identity, is part of nature. He is a
biological organism, subject like all other creatures to the
laws of nature. This implies that he is constantly affected by
his physical environment. Each of us is dependent on it, not
only for the material necessities of life (though that is the
one relationship most of us recognize) but for health and for
the balanced functioning of our senses, and ultimately for
emotional well-being. The subjective relationship to the environment—how it affects our senses—is the one we know the
least about; but we are beginning to study it and recognize
its importance. We know that sounds and lights and forms
and colors and movements and the other living organisms
in our environment influence, for better or worse, our
psychological and physical condition; this is merely another
aspect of our participation in nature.

There should be no misunderstanding at this juncture
of the importance of the city. No one is suggesting that a
man-made environment is inherently unnatural; no one is
advising a return to more primitive ways of living. On the
contrary, the city is (or should be) an environment where
certain natural influences operate unimpeded by others. If
it is not "unnatural" when creatures dig or build themselves
shelters to provide the kind of small-scale environment they

need, then it is not "unnatural" for us to build cities for the
same purpose. There is merely one condition attached, a
perfectly sensible one: that the man-made environment satisfy our native physical and psychological requirements. So
the job of the urbanist and architect is essentially to design a
man-made environment which is as natural as possible.

The forum on the problems of the expanding metropolis
(and its kindred gatherings) is an indication, if any were
needed, that we have not been successful of late in making
these environments. There is one obvious reason for our
failure: we are now building on a vast scale where instinct and
tradition no longer provide any reliable guidance. Instinctive
knowledge, invaluable under certain conditions, ceases to be
useful when it is a question of organizing a modern industrial city or operating a ten-thousand acre farm, and we have
to acquire knowledge of a different sort. In a sense, that is
what the forum is trying to do. But there is another reason
for our failure: during the last century and a half we have
persisted in separating man from nature and in keeping them
separate. The separation I mean is not primarily a physical
one, an inevitable outcome of modern urban existence; it is a
separation incorporated in our dichotomous way of thinking.
It is a nineteenth-century aberration and in time it will pass.
One element of the urban population flees to the greener,
more virtuous, more "natural" suburbs, while the planners
and developers and social technicians dream of rebuilding
the city on a sumptuous scale with purely social and economic
objectives. Both parties give up all attempts to recreate an
efficient man-made environment, and the city as a cultural
achievement is threatened with extinction. The symbiotic
minded observer can tell us why: the modern city may
be rich and efficient and intellectually vital, but it has ceased

to insure health and a sense of well-being; it has ceased
to be a natural environment.

Remedies at Hand

Now there would be little point in repeating a familiar in-
dictment if there were no alternatives available; but there are.
There are signs in many directions of fresh thinking on the
problem; hints of possible solutions to be found in precisely
those quarters which are not represented at the forum. Iron-
ically enough, it is the countryside which can best teach us
how to recreate the objective natural environment in the city,
for in the American rural landscape it is already possible to
see or sense a new concept of the environment based on
the premise of the interdependence of contrary; a man-made
environment—house, farm, or city, all forms of life. Brand-
new towns and cities are a dime a dozen; they are admit-
tedly more exciting to visit than an experimental farm or an
agricultural station or a laboratory, and when we think of
the new landscape we think of new communities. But after
we have inspected and admired a few of them they begin to
pall; even the most modern and most ingeniously planned
prove to be little more than replicas of the old, with the
same old emphasis on the social, the same old disregard of
the environment. This is not true of agriculture; unlike urbanism, it has had to learn the hard way that the old philosophy is inadequate. Whether large-scale mechanized farms are
economically and socially desirable is open to debate; but they
have certainly inspired a vast amount of new study of the relationship between environment and organic life. Soils, crops,
livestock, even forests and streams are no longer thought
of by intelligent farmers entirely in terms of yield; they are

recognized as inseparable elements in a complex biological-meteorological system. City dwellers know little of the men who are making these discoveries: the ecologists, climatologists, agronomists, soil and water experts, botanists, entomologists, veterinarians working in a score of agricultural colleges and research institutions; they know even less of what they are doing. But what these scientists are finding out will eventually concern every one of us, and in the meantime they are helping transform the rural landscape, and the thinking and behavior of rural populations all over the world.

Most of their studies come under the heading of climate and include the effect of temperature, barometric pressure, wind, sunlight, radiation, rainfall—in their daily and seasonal manifestations—on organic life. All of these factors influence human health and efficiency, and we are constantly adjusting to them, whether we are aware of it or not. Thanks to those rural experiments, we now know a great deal about the action of climate on man, and the action of man on the micro-climate, the climate of cities. We know that every time we heap up a mass of masonry or cut through a hill or drain a swamp or plant a row of trees or fill the air with smoke or pave an open area we are to some extent changing the local climate, the local environment, and changing our own physical condition. It is merely a question of putting this knowledge to intelligent use in the design of cities. In the most literal sense of the word, it is elementary knowledge, and the public is becoming increasingly aware of it. That is why it is puzzling to note how little the average urbanist seems to care about the climate he is unwittingly creating, or about how it can be controlled. He still seems to think that it is enough to pay passing respect to the importance of sunlight and fresh air, and to refer to parks as the "lungs of the city." This may have been heady stuff in Le Corbusier's heyday, but any modern farmer knows more about the complexities of climate than that, and more about its potentialities.

This much, therefore, we can easily learn from the natural scientists about how to make our cities at once more natural and more humane. A properly planned climate and proper protective measures are essential to the new city; but that is by no means all that we must have; the physical environment determines more than our organic health; and if the urbanist considers nature merely a spectacle—preferably in the form of open green spaces—we would be guilty of the same sort of error if we thought of it merely as a prophylactic agent.

Subjective Nature

Our basic concept of the world, of the environment, comes through our senses, and it is by means of the senses that we judge whether it is good or bad. The environment must of course be designed to promote harmonious social relationships, just as it must be designed to promote our physical well-being, but it must also be designed to stimulate our sight and hearing and sense of touch and smell. We are accustomed to look for these pleasures in the green outdoors where, to be sure, they are present in their purest and most immediate form; but the need for a satisfying sensory experience is with us no matter where we are, and nowhere is that experience more intense (though not always more agreeable) than in the modern city. We have all been educated to ignore, or at least to minimize, the testimony of our senses, to rationalize our sensory reactions in social or ethical or

formal aesthetic terms; and this is particularly true of the
urban environment. Yet it is not unlikely that much of the
enjoyment we derive from exploring a foreign city, whose
social and historical background is unfamiliar to us, is primarily sensory: an indefinable but very real delight in a novel
sequence of lights, colors, spaces, sounds, and forms. New
York City offers a conspicuous example of a rich and almost
completely satisfactory sensory experience: Grand Central
Terminal. It is entirely proper to analyze its interior as formal architecture or (what is today more fashionable) as an
organization of space for certain collective activities, and in
any final appraisal of the building those two aspects have to
be included. But to the average man the immediate experience of Grand Central is neither architectural nor social;
it is sensory. He passes through a marvelous sequence;
emerging in a dense, slow-moving crowd from the dark, cool,
low-ceilinged platform, he suddenly enters the immense
concourse with its variety of heights and levels, its spacious-
ness, its acoustical properties, its diffused light, and the
smooth texture of its floors and walls. Almost every sense is
stimulated and flattered; even posture and gait are momen-
tarily improved. Few other cities can offer such a concentra-
tion of delights; certainly Paris has nothing comparable. The
nearest equivalent is the Vienna *Hofburg* with its succession
of open places and dark arcades, its tremendous panorama
of city and mountains abruptly alternating with intimate
architectural areas.

Such man-made complexes are imitation of landscapes;
at their best they provide us with something of the stimulation we get from a brief walk through a valley among trees
and open fields; they satisfy for the time being our craving
for contact with a variety of forms and spaces and lights and

sounds. Unfortunately the tendency of the past century has been to eliminate every natural sight, sound, and color from the urban scene; State Street in Chicago is typical of what we now have left. In one respect it is a brilliant show; in another it represents almost complete impoverishment. When we walk along it our hearing and our instinctive feel for the proper interval between human bodies are affronted by the noise and the crowds; a monotonous dead-level surface is underfoot, and a monotonous geometric perspective stretches in either direction; monotonous façades rise on either side. The signs and window displays, often defended for the variety and visual stimulation they offer, are actually addressed to a totally different aspect of our vision; they are meant to be read and interpreted, rather than to be seen.

Far more of our time and energy are spent in the unconscious pursuit of these sensory experiences than we realize. The view from a height, the sudden glimpse of an expanse of sky or water or city, the unobscured light, the sound of human beings at play, the color and texture of flowers and lawns, the protective enclosed space, or the stream of activity —these are what we are always seeking, because something tells us that they are vital to us. The contemporary city frustrates those desires; the city which the average urbanist dreams of satisfies only incidentally; but it is encouraging to see that more and more attention is being given to them—or at least to their investigation.

Research is underway in the layout of highways and expressways to provide a variety of visual experiences, not only for the pleasure of drivers but to keep their attention alert. From all corners comes evidence that we are beginning to understand the bond between the outside world and our subconscious inner world. Aircraft companies, the armed

forces, and such organizations as the Acoustical Society of
America are investigating bio-acoustics and subjective acous-
tics; the effect, for instance, of intense sound on our sense
of time and of balance, and on our health. To date, these
findings have been used chiefly in the suppression of noise
in industry and transportation, but to the imaginative planner and architect they offer the possibility of creating pleasant acoustical environments anywhere in the city. We could,
if we chose, design areas where human sounds predominated;
we could (as they have already done in Scandinavia) plan
and design dwellings with an acoustical restful and relaxed
atmosphere. We still have to learn about our color environment, though Madison Avenue is investigating it after its
own fashion, and we have still to provide satisfactory stimulation for the muscular sense; the urban landscape is full
of immovable, untouchable objects.

The Sociological Obsession

We would be much nearer applying this knowledge to the
creation of an agreeable man-made natural environment were
it not for our tendency to misinterpret our sensory needs.
Every American is an amateur sociologist, inclined to believe
that any desire can be finally satisfied by social measures.
At the moment he sees "status seeking" wherever he looks:
in our love for high-powered cars, our flight to the suburbs,
the popularity of patio living and of winter sports. He cannot
believe that these tastes possibly represent nothing more
complicated than attempts to experience freedom in space
or movement in a fresh and stimulating way. The status
seeking motive is important, perhaps more important in
many cases than the other; and yet even a slight recognition

of our perennial search for sensory experiences would help us see many problems in a new light. We would for example recognize that a significant aspect of juvenile delinquency was its rebellion against a hostile, unnatural physical environment, against ugly sounds and smells and colors; houses and streets and cities designed for efficiency but not for highly sensitive biological organisms. We would also recognize that our instinctive preference for certain urban environments had an aesthetic-sensory rather than a social basis. Much has recently been said about the charms of the neighborhood as contrasted with the vast impersonality of the metropolis, and it is suggested that we return to the neighborhood pattern of living. Can we be entirely sure that these charms are not actually a matter of small scale and acoustical intimacy and slower movement? After the noise and rush of the surrounding city nothing can be more refreshing than a glimpse of such an environment; but do we necessarily want to live in it? *Must* we interpret every aspect of the city in terms of domesticity?

The well-designed city is one where we everywhere feel at home; it reminds us, everywhere and at all times, that we are in an environment no less natural, no less stimulating than the environment of the country dweller. Its trees and parks and lawns are more than agents of health; they tell us of the passage of the seasons, and its open places tell us the time of day. If the well-designed city cannot provide us with contact with other forms of life it provides us with the society of other human beings in places designed for relaxation; if it cannot provide us with the sounds of the remoter landscape it at least provides us with areas where the sound of human voices and footsteps are not drowned out by mechanical noises, it provides us with quiet. It cannot imitate all of nature, but it gives us archways and pools of daylight, and flights of steps and views; the splash of water in fountains, echoes and music; the breath of damp cool air, the harmony of colors and the unpolluted sun; indeed it gives us so much that our excursions into the countryside cease to be headlong flights from a sterile environment, and become a conscious searching for the missing ingredients: solitude in the presence of other forms of life, space, and mystery.

As a man-made environment every city has three functions to fulfill: it must be a just and efficient social institution; it must be a biologically wholesome habitat; and it must be a continuously satisfying aesthetic-sensory experience. Up to the present we have given all thought to the first of these. There are signs that the second will receive its due attention before long; for it is already outside the city gates. But the third will be realized only when we ourselves are enlightened: when we learn once again to see nature in its entirety; not as a remote object to be worshipped or ignored as it suits us, but as part of ourselves.

Images of the City

SHEDDING A discrete tear over the demolition of the ornamental plazas at both ends of the Manhattan Bridge—they
are or were handsome semi-circular colonnades somewhat
in the manner of John Barrington Bayley's dreams of a neo-
Baroque metropolis—the *New York Times** observed that
the city is inimical to public works of art on a relatively
human scale. Why? Because "New York has grown like
some giant crystal in a pattern formed by the constriction
of the space in which the components are deposited," the
editorial explained. "Unlike a work of art, the city is
anonymous and impersonal; its spectacular form, although
composed of an infinite number of man-designed units, is
self-determined."

Neatly put; and the *Times* continued in the same geological
vein: "Seen from a distance or from the air, the city is like
a new natural phenomenon, created not by the tensions of
the earth's crust that forces up mountains, or by the erosion
that modifies their forms, but by the economic circumstances
that thrust skyscrapers into the air and by the problems
of human existence that have channeled routes to and
through them. The demolition of the two plazas is, from
this point of view, as inevitable and as natural as erosion in
Nature."

Here we actually have a choice of two ingenious similes:
the city as a crystal, fulfilling a mysteriously preordained
pattern, and the city as a kind of mountain landscape—tene-

[From *Landscape*, Vol. 11, No. 1, Autumn 1961]
* Editorial, June 7, 1961.

ments, department stores, office buildings slowly, majestically
heaving out of the earth in reponse to an irresistible force,
only to be divided and worn down and finally reduced to
rubble by the incessant passage of trucks, buses, taxis, by
the busy feet of commuters, shoppers, policemen, Western
Union messengers. While we cannot vouch for the geological
accuracy of the comparison, we recognize and admire its
cosmic quality. In the past, in order to emphasize the
antihuman aspects of the city, critics have been content
to liken it to a wen, to an octopus, to a cancer, to hell; how
much to be preferred is the *Times*'s comparing New York to
a man-made mountain range, solemnly burying itself in its
own avalanches!

It is usually the detached spectator of the city—the planner
or urban geographer or sociologist—who sees it primarily
in terms of flux and change: these similes of multiplying cells,
of encircling tentacles, of increasing communication loads, of
floods and erosion correspond to *his* notion of the essential
urban landscape—a landscape of movement and perpetual
aimless growth. But does the city dweller himself understand the city in these terms? Does he want to understand
it in these terms? We have our doubts. It is easy to admire
a man-made mountain range and to boast of its highest peaks,
but are we likely to choose to live and raise a family in any
of the more notorious landslide areas? If every event—the
destruction of a monument suddenly become too small, the
destruction of a park suddenly become an obstacle to traffic
—is, in the words of the *Times*, natural and inevitable, what
point is there in trying to play a decisive role in the city's
life? And it is not probable that many persons would willingly pay taxes for the maintenance of a mountain range

which is inevitably and naturally eroding itself—and them—
out of existence.

The geological simile demands that we view the city from
a distance or from the air, just as the biological simile demands that we see it through a microscope. But for most
New Yorkers their city is seen through a windshield, from
a bedroom window, from a crowded sidewalk; on the way
to school, to the office, to the drugstore. The Alpine perspective (and indeed the microscopic perspective) may inspire the artist, but the citizen is inspired—if that is the
word for his reaction—by confronting the city on a strictly
human level.

That is why there still seems something to be said for
those human allegories of states and cities—Columbia, Bri-
tannia, Lutetia, Berolina, Pallas Athene. Remnants of a forgotten mythology, now surviving chiefly as convenient clichés
for political cartoonists, they once provided the townsman
with a vivid image of the society he lived in. The classically
garbed female divinity had her shortcomings; the array of
obsolete weapons and implements—swords, scales, crown
and torch and laurel branch—was a way of defying all progress, and the tight steel breastplate sternly repudiated the
notion of urban sprawl. But an affront to her dignity was
something easily understood and resented in common human
terms. The stripping of two ornaments (in the form of monumental plazas) from such a figure would have been an action
few officials would be bold enough to undertake.

We are already living in cities which can only be interpreted
in terms of electronic or bio-chemical models, and the devising of such models is one of the problems facing those
who are concerned with keeping our cities alive. But for most

of us the human image dies hard; destroy it in one place and we look for it in another. Perhaps the flight of many of us from the city to the suburbs is in part at least such a search: for a smaller, more understandable community: the village whose unchanging image is the superfamily.

The Stranger's Path

As ONE WHO is by way of being a professional tourist with a certain painfully acquired knowledge of how to appraise strange cities, I often find myself brought up short by citizens remarking that I can't really hope to *know* a town until I have seen the inside of one of its homes. I usually agree, expecting that there will then ensue an invitation to their house and a chance to admire one of these shrines of local culture, these epitomes of whatever it is the town or city has to offer. All that follows is an urgent suggestion that I investigate on my own the residential quarter before I presume to form a final opinion. "Ours is a city of homes," they add; "the downtown section is like that anywhere else, but our Country Club Heights" (or Snob Hill or West End or European Section or Villa Quarter, depending on where I am) "is considered unique."

I have accordingly set out to explore that part of the city, and many are the hours I have spent wandering through carefully labyrinthine suburbs, seeking to discover the *essential* city, as distinguished from that of the tourist or transient. In retrospect these districts all seem indistinguishable: tree- and garden-lined avenues and lanes, curving about a landscape of hills with pretty views over other hills; the traffic becomes sparser, the houses retreat further behind tall trees and expensive flowers; every prospect is green, most prosperous and beautiful. The latest model cars wait on the carefully raked driveway or at the immaculate curb, and there comes the sound of tennis being played. When evening falls, the softest, most domestic lights shine from upstairs windows;

[From *Landscape*, Vol. 7, No. 1, Autumn 1957]

the only reminder of the nearby city is that dusty pink glow in the sky which in any case the trees all but conceal.

Yet why have I always been glad to leave? Was it a painful realization that I was excluded from these rows and rows of (presumably) happy and comfortable homes that has always ended by making me beat a retreat to the city proper? Or was it a conviction that I had actually seen this, experienced it, relished it after a fashion countless times and could no longer derive the slightest spark of inspiration from it? Ascribe it if you like to a kind of sour grapes, but in the course of years of travel I have come to believe that in the home, the domestic establishment, far from being a unique symbol of the local way of life, is essentially the same wherever you go. The lovely higher income residential zone of Spokane is, I suspect, hardly to be distinguished (except for a few interesting but not very significant architectural variations) from the corresponding zone of Oslo or Naples or Rio de Janeiro. Granted the sanctity of the home, its social, cultural, biological importance, is it necessarily the truest index of a society? Offhand I would say the stranger could derive just as revealing an insight into a foreign way of life by listening to a country sermon or reading the classified ads in a popular newspaper or watching the behavior of a crowd during a street altercation—or for that matter by deciphering the graffiti on public walls.

At all events the home is not everything. The residential quarter, despite its undeniable charms, is not the entire city, and if we poor lonely travelers are ignorant of the joys of existence on Monte Vista Terrace and Queen Alexandra Lane we are on the other hand apt to know much more about some other aspects of the city than the life-long resident does. I am thinking in particular of that part of the city

devoted to the outsider, the transient, devoted to receiving
him and satisfying his immediate needs. I am possibly prone
to overemphasize this function of the city, for it is naturally
the one I see most of; but who is it, I'd like to know, who
keeps the city going, who makes it important to the outside
world: the permanent resident with his predictable tastes
and habits, or the stranger who brings money and business
and new ideas? Both groups, of course, are vital to the
community; their efforts are complementary; but there is a
peculiar tendency among us to think of the city as a self-
contained and even a sort of defensive unit, forever struggling
to keep its individuality intact. "Town" in English comes
from a Teutonic word meaning hedge or enclosure; strange
that this concept, obsolete a thousand years and more, should
somehow have managed to stow away and cross the Atlantic,
so that even in America we are reluctant to think of our
cities as places where strangers come; with us the resident
is always given preference. I gather it was quite the opposite
in ancient Egypt; there the suffix corresponding to "town"
or "ton" meant "The place one arrives at"—a notion I
much prefer.

Anyhow, regardless of our hesitation to think of our cities
as "places one arrives at" in pursuit of business or pleasure
or new ideas, that is actually what most of them are. Every
sizeable community exists partly to satisfy the outsider who
visits it. Not only that; there always evolves a special part of
town devoted to this purpose. What name to give this zone
of transients is something of a problem, for unlike the other
subdivisions of the city this one, I think, must be thought
of in terms of movement along a pretty well-defined axis.
For the stranger progresses up a reasonably predictable
route from his point of arrival to his final destination—and

then, of course, he is likely to retrace his steps. Call it a path, in the sense that it is a way not deliberately constructed or planned for that purpose. Actually the Stranger's Path is, in most cities, easily recognizable, once a few of its land-marks are known, and particularly (so I have found) in American cities of between say twenty and fifty thousand. Larger cities naturally possess a Stranger's Path of their own, but often it is so extensive and complex that it is exceedingly hard to define. As for towns of less than twenty thousand the Path here is rarely fully developed, so that it is equally difficult to trace. Thus the Path I am most familiar with is the one in the smaller American city.

Where it begins is easy enough to establish, for it is the place where the stranger first disembarks. You may object that this can be almost anywhere, but the average stranger still arrives by bus or train or truck, and even if he arrives in his own car he is likely to try and park somewhere out-side the more congested downtown area. Arrival therefore signifies a change in the means of transportation: from train or truck or car to something else, and this transfer is likely to take place either at the station or the bus depot. Near these establishments (and for a variety of obvious reasons) you will also find the truck centers, the larger parking lots, and even a taxi stand or two.

So the beginning of the Path is marked by the abandoned means of transportation and the area near the railroad tracks. We are welcomed to the city by a smiling landscape of park-ing lots, warehouses, pot-holed and weedgrown streets where isolated filling stations and quick lunch counters are scattered among cinders like survivals of a bombing raid. But where does the path lead from here? Directly to the center of town? To the hotels or the civic center or the main street?

Not necessarily, and I believe we can only begin to follow
the stranger's progress into the city when we have found
out who these strangers are and what they are after. There
are cities, to be sure, where most transients are well-heeled
tourists and pleasure seekers; Las Vegas, Nevada, is one,
and Monte Carlo is another; so are countless other resort
towns all over the globe. The Path in such places usually
leads to a hotel. But stranger does not always mean tourist,
and by and large the strangers who come to town for a day
or two belong to a more modest class: not very prosperous,
often with no money at all. They are men looking for a
job or on their way to a job; men come to buy or sell one
item in their line of business, men on a brief holiday. In
terms of cash outlay in the local stores no very brilliant
public; in terms of labor and potential skills, in terms of
experience of other ways of doing things, or other ways of
thinking, a very valuable influx indeed. Besides, is it not one
of the chief functions of the city to exchange as well as to
receive? Furthermore, the greater part of these strangers
would seem to be unattached men from some smaller town
or from the country. These characteristics are worth bearing
in mind, for they make the Path in the average small city
what it now is: loud, tawdry, down at the heel, full of dives
and small catch-penny businesses, and (in the eyes of the
uptown residential white-collar element) more than a little
shady and dangerous.

Some urban geographer will be able to explain why the
Stranger's Path becomes more respectable the further it gets
from its point of origin; why the flophouses and brothels
and the poorest among the second-hand shops (now euphe-
mistically called loan establishments—the three golden balls
are a thing of the past), the dirtiest and steamiest of Greasy

Spoons tend to cluster around those first raffish streets near
the depot and bus and truck terminals, and why the city's
finest hotel, its most luxurious night club, its largest restaurant with a French name and illustrated menus are all at
the other end. But so it is; one terminus of the Path is Skid
Row, the other is the local Great White Way, and remote
though they seem from each other they are still organically
and geographically linked. The moral is clear: the Path caters
to every pocketbook, every taste, and what gives it its uni-
fying quality and sets it off from the rest of the city is its
eagerness to satisfy the unattached man from out of town,
here either for a brief bout of pleasure or on some business
errand.

Still, it would be foolish to maintain that the Path is everywhere identical; somewhere between its extremes, one of
squalor, the other of opulence, it achieves its most characteristic and vigorous aspect, and it is in this middle region of
the Path that the town seems to display all that it has to offer
the outsider, though in a crude form. The City as Place of
Exchange: such a definition in the residential section, even
in the section devoted to public institutions, would seem
incongruous, but here you learn its validity. Nearby on a
converging street or in a square you find the local produce
market. It is not so handsome and prosperous as it once was,
for except in the more varied farming regions of the United
States it has dwindled to a weekly display of potted plants
and fryers and a few seasonal vegetables; Lancaster, Pennsylvania, has a noteworthy exception. But still the market,
even in its reduced state, survives in most of the small cities
I have visited, and it continues to serve as a center for a
group of feed and grain stores, hardware stores, and an
occasional tractor and implement agency. Here in fact is

another one of those transshipment points; the streets surrounding the market are crowded with farm trucks, and with
farmers setting out to explore the Path. Exchange is taking
place everywhere you look: exchange of goods for cash, exchange of labor for cash (or the promise of cash) in the em-
ployment agencies with their opportunities scrawled in chalk
on blackboards; exchange of talk and drink and opinion in
a dozen bars and beer parlors and lunch counters; exchange
of mandolins and foreign pistols and diamond rings against
cash—to be exchanged in turn against an hour or so with a
girl. The Path bursts into a luxuriance of colored and lighted
signs: CHILIBURGERS. RED HOTS. UNBORN CALF OXFORDS:
THEY'RE NEW! THEY'RE SMART! THEY'RE IVY! DOUBLE FEATURE:
BRIDE OF THE GORILLA—MONSTER FROM OUTER SPACE. GOSPEL
EVANGELICAL MISSION. CHECKS CASHED. SNOOKER PARLOR. THE
BEST SHINE IN TOWN! DR. LOGAN AND HIS AMAZING EURO-
PATHIC METHOD. CONEY ISLANDS. FORTUNES TOLD; MADAME
LAFAY. And Army surplus stores, tattoo parlors, barbershops,
poolrooms lined with pinball and slot machines, gift shops
with Chinese embroidered coats and tea sets. Along one Path
after another—in Paducah and Vicksburg and Poplar Bluff
and Quincy—I have run across, to my amazement, strange
little establishments (wedged in perhaps between a hotel with
only a dark flight of steps on the street and a luggage store
going out of business) where they sell joke books and party
favors and comic masks—worthy reminders that the Path,
for all its stench of beer and burning grease, its bleary eyes
and uncertain clutching of doorjams, its bedlam of jukeboxes
and radios and barkers, is still dedicated to good times. And
in fact the Path is at its gayest and noisiest and most popular
from Saturday noon until midnight.

   You may call this part of town what you like: Skid Row,

the Jungle, the Tenderloin, Hell's Kitchen, or (in the loftier parlance of sociology) a depressed or obsolescent area; but you cannot accurately call it a slum. It is, as I have said, primarily a district for unattached men from out of town. This implies a minority of unattached women, but it does not imply that any families live here. No children are brought up here, no home has to struggle against the atmosphere of anarchy. That is why you find no grocery or household furniture or womens' and children's clothing stores, though stores with gifts for women are numerous enough. Not being an urban morphologist, I have no inkling of *why* there are no slum dwellings here, nor, for that matter, of where in the city makeup slums are likely to occur; but I have yet to find anywhere even the remotest connection between an extensive slum area and the Strangers' Path.

But then there is much in the whole matter that mystifies me. I cannot understand why loan establishments always exist cheek by jowl with the large and pretentious small city bank buildings; why the Path merges almost without transition into the financial section of the city. Yet I have observed this too often to be entirely mistaken. Scollay Square in Boston was not far from State Street, the Bowery is not far (in metropolitan terms) from Wall Street, and Chicago's Skid Row, the classic of them all, is only a few blocks from the center of the financial district; and nowhere is there a a slum between the two extremes. I imagine the connection here is one easily explained in terms of the nineteenth-century American city and its exchange function; perhaps the Path was originally a link between warehouse and counting house, between depot and Main Street. And there are other traits I find equally hard to fathom: why the Path rarely if ever touches on the fashionable retail district or the culturally conscious civic center with its monument and museum and library and welfare organizations housed in remodelled old mansions. These two parts of town are of course the favorite haunts of the residents of the city; is that why the Path avoids all contact with them?

When the Path has reached the region of banks and hotels —usually grouped around one or two intersections in the average small city—it has lost much of its loud proletarian quality, and about all that is left is a newsstand with out-of-town papers, a travel agency, and an airline office on the ground floor of the dressy hotel. Here at one of the busiest corners it seems to pause and hesitate: Main Street leads to the substantial older residential district and eventually (if you're persistent and ambitious enough) to beautiful restricted Country Club Heights. Broadway is the beginning of the retail shopping district. The Path finally makes its way to City Hall; and here it is, among the surrounding decrepit brick office buildings dating from the last century that it touches upon another and final aspect of the city: the politico-legal. Lawyers, the legal aid society, bonding companies, insurance agents, a new (but no less rapacious) breed of finance establishments proliferate among dark wainscoted corridors and behind transoms in high-ceilinged rooms. With a kind of artistic appropriateness, the initial hangdog atmosphere of the depot and flophouse reasserts itself around the last landmark on the Path, the City Hall. Groups of hastily sobered-up faces gather forlornly outside the traffic court and the police court, or on the steps of the City Hall itself, while grimy documents are passed about. From across the street the YMCA, the Salvation Army, the Guild of Temperance Women look on benevolently, wanting to make friends but never quite succeeding. The Red Cross, on the

other hand, dwells in proud seclusion in the basement of the
Federal Building, several blocks away.

Is it in this manner that the Stranger's Path comes to an
end? If so, how sad, and how pointed the moral: start your
career in brothels and saloons and you wind up, hat in hand,
before the police magistrate. But this is not invariably the
case, and for all I have been able to discover the path (or
some portion of it) may go on to other, happier goals. Yet it is
here that it ceases to be a distinct feature of the urban landscape; from now on it is dispersed among all the other cur-
rents of city life. And the simile which inevitably comes to
mind is that of a river, a stream; a powerful, muddy, untidy but immensely fertile stream which, after being joined
by its tributaries, briefly cuts its own characteristic channel
in the gaudy middle section of its course, then, arrived at
the center of town, fans out to deposit its waters and their
burden, and vanishes.

There are two reasons for my trying to describe this part
of the average American city that I have called the Stranger's
Path; First, I wanted to show the people of that city that
while they may know the residential section and be immensely
proud of it, there is probably something about the downtown
section (something very valuable in its way) that they have
never recognized. My second reason is that I have derived
much pleasure from exploring the Path and learning a few
of its landmarks; hours in unknown cities that might otherwise have been dull thereby became enjoyable. And indeed
every city has such a section; there are remains of it among
the ruins of Pompeii; it was an integral part of every medie-
val town, and I have run across it in its clearest form in
Mexico and in the Balkans.

But what many people will ask is, how important is the
Stranger's Path to the modern city? What sort of a future
does it have? To such questions I can give no educated
answer. When I likened it to a river I was using no very
original simile, yet a simile having the virtue of aptness and
of suggesting two characteristics. The Path, as I see it, has
the prime function of introducing new life to the city, of
bringing the city into touch with the outside world. (That it
also has the no less valuable function of bringing the villager,
the lonely field worker or traveling salesman or trucker or
the inhabitant of a dehumanized commercial farming landscape into touch with urban culture goes without saying.)
Granted that these contacts are not always on a very ex-
alted or even worthwhile scale, and that they are increasingly
confined to the lowest class of citizen; nevertheless they are
what keep an infinite number of small businesses and arts and
crafts alive, and they represent what is after all one of the
chief purposes of the city: the serving as a place of general
exchange. For my part I cannot conceive of any large community surviving without this ceaseless influx of new wants,
new ideas, new manners, new strength, and so I cannot conceive of a city without some section corresponding to the
Path.

The simile was further that of a stream which empties into no basin or lake, merely evaporating into the city or perhaps rising to the surface once more outside of town along
some highway strip; and it is this lack of a final, well-defined
objective that prevents the Path from serving an even more
important role in the community and that tends to make it
a poor man's district. For when the stranger, the transient,
has finished his business, something in the layout of the city
should invite him to linger and become part of the town,

should impel him to pay his respects, as it were. In other
words the Path should open into the center of civic leisure,
into a square or plaza where citizens gather.

"Well," says the city planner, "we have given that matter
some thought. We have decided to demolish the depressed
area of the city (including your so-called Path where the
financial return is low, the sanitation bad, and the traffic
hopeless) and erect a wonderful series of apartment houses
for moderate income white-collar workers, who are the back-
bone of our country. We will landscape the development
with wading pools, flagstone walks, groves of Chinese elms,
and we are also putting in a series of neighborhood shopping
centers. And that is not all," he continues enthusiastically;
"the City Hall is being removed, a handsome park will take
its place with parking facilities for five hundred cars under-
neath, and *more* shops, as high class as possible, will be built
around the square." He then goes on to talk about the pedestrian traffic-free center, with frequent references to the
Piazza San Marco in Venice.

All well and good; freedom from traffic is what we want,
and no one can object to a pretty square where none existed
before. But I am growing a little weary of the Piazza San
Marco. I yield to no one in my admiration of its beauty
and social utility, but it seems to me that those who hold it
up as the prototype of all civic (traffic-free) centers are not
always aware of what makes it what it is. The Piazza is not
an area carved out of a residential district; its animation
comes not from the art monuments which surround it; on
the contrary, it is enclosed on three sides by a maze of streets
and alleys whose function is almost exactly that of the Path;
moreover the Piazza San Marco has a landing-place where
farmers, fishermen, sailors, merchants and travelers all first

disembark—or used to disembark—in the city. These prosaic characteristics are what gives life to it. And then, how
about the *universal* absence of wheeled traffic in Venice? The
Mediterranean plaza is a charming and healthy institution,
which American cities would be wise to adopt, but the plaza
is organically connected with the workaday life of the city.
It has never served, it was never intended to serve, as a place
of business. It is the center of group leisure; it is the civic
parlor and it therefore adjoins the civic workroom or place
of exchange. The notion of a pedestrian plaza in the center
of every small American city is a good one, but if it is merely
to serve as a focal point for smart shops and "culture" then
I still do not see in it any substitute for the Path.

    There are others who try to persuade us that the suburban
or residential shopping center is the civic center of the future.
Mr. Victor Gruen, who is justifiably happy over his enormous
(and enormously successful) shopping centers in Detroit
and Minneapolis, tells us that these establishments (or
rather their handsomely landscaped surroundings) are already
serving more and more as the scene of holiday festivities,
art shows, pageants, as well as of general sociability and
of supervised play for children. I have no doubt of it; but
the shopping center, no matter how big, how modern,
how beautiful, is the *exact* opposite of the Path. Its public
is almost exclusively composed of housewives and children,
it imposes a uniformity of taste and income and interests,
and its strenuous efforts to be self-contained mean that it
automatically rejects anything from outside. And compared
to any traditional civic center—marketplace, bazaar, agora—
what bloodless places these shopping centers are! I cannot
see a roustabout fresh from the oil fields, or (at the other
extreme) a student of manners willingly passing an hour in

one of them; though both could spend a day and a night in the Path with pleasure and a certain amount of profit. Art shows indeed! It strikes me that some of our planners need to acquire a more robust idea of city life. Perhaps I do them an injustice, but I often have the feeling that their emphasis on convenience, cleanliness, and safety, their distrust of everything vulgar and small and poor is symptomatic of a very lopsided view of urban culture.

Possibly this is the price we have to pay for planning becoming respectable, but it would be well if a wider and more humane understanding of the city and its problem soon evolved in this country. There is much to be done, and planners are the only ones who can do it. No one, I suppose, would wish to see the Stranger's Path remain as it is: garish and dirty and decaying, forced to expend its vitality in mean and neglected streets, cheated of a final merger with the broader life of the city. Yet even in its present sad state it has the power to suggest the avenue it might become, given imaginative treatment. Among the famous and best loved streets of the world how many of them are simply glorifications of the Stranger's Path! The Rambla in Barcelona, more than a mile of tree-lined boulevard with more trees and a promenade down the center, is such a one, and the Cannebière in Marseilles is another. They both link the harbor (the point of arrival) with the uptown area; neither of them is a show street in terms of architecture, and they are not bordered by expensive or fashionable shops. The public which frequents them at every hour of the day and night is not a "class" public; it is composed of a large cross section of the population of the city, men, women, and children, rich and poor, strangers and natives. It happens that the residential section of both of these cities contain architectural wonders

which must be visited: Gaudi's church in Barcelona, and
Le Corbusier's Cité Radieuse in Marseilles, and here (as in
so many other places) I have done my duty, only to return
as fast as possible to the center of town and those marvelous
avenues.

There are few greater delights than to walk up and down
them in the evening along with thousands of other people;
up and down, relishing the lights coming through the trees
or shining from the façades, listening to the sounds of music
and foreign voices and traffic, enjoying the smell of flowers
and good food and the air from the nearby sea. The sidewalks are lined with small shops, bars, stalls, dance halls,
movies, booths lighted by acetylene lamps, and everywhere
are strange faces, strange costumes, strange and delightful
impressions. To walk up such a street into the quieter, more
formal part of town, is to be part of a procession, part of a
ceaseless ceremony of being initiated into the city and of
rededicating the city itself. And that is how our first progress through even the smallest city and town should be: a
succession of gay and beautiful streets and squares, all of
them extending a universal welcome.

Unlike so many visions of the city of the future this one
has a firm basis in reality. The Stranger's Path exists in one
form or another in every large community, either (as in most
American cities) ignored, or, as in the case of Marseilles and
Barcelona and many other cities in the Old World, preserved
and cherished. Everywhere it is the direct product of our
economic and social evolution. If we seek to dam or bury
this ancient river, we will live to regret it.

Two Street Scenes

NUMBER ONE: Main Street, once planted with elms and possessing broad sidewalks, has been entirely transformed. First
one row of trees was chopped down, then the other, and
finally the sidewalks were reduced by half. Now the street
accommodates six lanes of traffic instead of three. Whatever
was left of the street's original character has been destroyed
by two recent municipal ordinances: one forbids parking
during business hours, the other makes it a one-way street.
Another street, parallel to Main, has been made one way
in the opposite direction.

The result, technologically speaking, is most impressive.
It is true that the property owners and merchants along
Main Street don't like it and that the public is a little uneasy without knowing why; but traffic experts and safety
engineers and trucking executives and city officials come
from far and wide to see how Main Street has been improved.

A tide of buses and trucks and passenger cars, usually five
abreast, surges through the heart of the city at twenty to
twenty-five miles per hour, eight hours a day. The authorities hope to increase this speed by one means or another.
Meanwhile they have installed clusters of overhead traffic
lights, equipped with gongs, at every intersection. The sidewalk corners have been chained off to prevent pedestrians
from crossing diagonally. Jaywalkers are handed summonses
by the police and in addition are given a brief memorized
sermon on the hazards of crossing against the lights. Once

[From *Landscape*, Vol. 3, No. 3, Spring 1954]

a year the Junior Chamber of Commerce, to show its zeal
for the public good, hires a comedian-acrobat to put on a
show at high noon at the intersection of Main and First
Streets. The public pauses to watch the clown dodge in and
out among the moving cars, vault over the hoods, collapse
on the bumpers and so on; a good half hour of laughs and
chills. The crowd disperses, temporarily scornful of any
pedestrian who would interfere with the flow of traffic by
jaywalking.

When the lights change there is a clanging of bells, and
the occasional sound of a policeman's whistle; cars which
have been delayed a second in their getaway make a furious
bleating. Then the cataract resumes. Sharp-eyed policemen
watch the flow, either from the curb or on motorcycles, and
usually a police car, with a two-way radio and a traffic expert on the front seat, cruises down-stream to make sure
that nothing occurs to interrupt or slow down the steady flow
of vehicles. It is all extremely well managed.

How fares it with the pedestrian on Main Street? An
unusual question. If he stays to the right of the sidewalk,
conforms to the average rate of progress, runs when the lights
are about to change; if he does not loiter or turn around
or try to walk abreast of someone else; generally speaking,
if he behaves like an automaton he will get along sufficiently
well. Actually he has learned not to expect any pleasure from
walking down Main Street; he is not likely to do more than
proceed straight ahead until he reaches his destination. There
are few distractions left in this part of town, though there
used to be plenty. The trees are gone, the benches where
there were streetcar stops are gone. City ordinances, widely
approved at the time, have forbidden any beggars or musi-
cians or vendors or shoeshine boys or pushcarts from appear-

ing in the down-town area. All commercial displays must be behind glass and even window displays must not be of a nature to attract crowds and thus slow up traffic. For some reason the merchants seek to attract the attention of the passing motorist and not that of the passing pedestrian; so almost all the signs are above the street level.

During work hours street and sidewalk are crowded; after work hours they are all but empty. A few cars hurtle down the deserted traffic-way with its succession of blinking yellow lights at the intersections. A few pedestrians, headed for a show or a restaurant, park their car and hurry to a side street. The store windows are dark. The only color and gaiety comes from the electric and neon lights half way up the façades. Main Street, within the memory of man, was once the center of the city. Transformed and streamlined to satisfy special interests, it has now destroyed most of the city's communal outdoor life, and frightened away the remainder.

NUMBER TWO: This Main Street, far older and far narrower than the other, is always hopelessly congested. It always has been during its more than three centuries of existence and it always will be. It and the nearby square constitute the very heart of the town and its corporate life. Main Street leads nowhere; it merely exists.

At nine A.M. there is a wedding in the cathedral. A hooting procession of some ten cars, all festooned with ribbons and streamers comes down Main Street, paying no attention to traffic lights, and goes twice around the square, making as much noise and being as conspicuously happy as possibly. Everyone pauses to watch, and finds some comment to make. Traffic may have been temporarily paralyzed, but the stock of public pleasure and wisdom has been greatly increased. At eleven A.M. there is another wedding with precisely the same effect.

At three P.M. the high school stages a homecoming celebration in the form of a parade twice the length of Main Street and once around the square. Twenty-five cars, six trucks with bands or floats and adorned with aggressive slogans alternate with groups of cheering and singing students. The parade passes at ten miles per hour; the air reeks of scorched brake linings and exhaust. An even younger public watches enviously from the sidewalk. While this is going on all traffic comes to a dead stop. Drivers wait with a greater or lesser degree of patience and goodwill, but they wait, and whether they relish it or not for the time being they are involved in the life of the community.

Throughout the day (and much of the night) there are groups of idlers on every corner crossing whenever and wherever they please to pass the time of day with friends loitering on another corner. There are shoeshine boys, a fraudulent begger or two, Indians selling blankets; wife and child squat on the nearby sidewalk and placidly consume a picnic lunch. There are cars stopping and backing to greet a passerby. Pedestrians and motorists are on the most cordial terms. On occasion the street is roped off after dark for dancing or a band concert.

Far from becoming subdued when the work day is done, Main Street and the square are at their liveliest from five o'clock on, and what's more, the life is chiefly pedestrian.

Now the first of these scenes is in almost any small American city which has the fortune (or misfortune) to be situated on an important freight highway and to possess a city council that likes to try to solve traffic problems for the exclusive benefit of the motorist. The second happens to be in Santa

Fe, New Mexico. But the essential contrast between the two kinds of street is not that between industrial and non-industrial communities or even that between coherent and incoherent city plans. It is the contrast between those communities which with the best of intentions have allowed their streets to be used and planned almost exclusively for heavy and rapid through traffic, and a community where the streets are still common property, still part of the living space of every citizen. It is not too much to say that there is pageantry of a sort in the streets of Santa Fe, whereas there is none in the streets of the average American city of today.

Many factors have helped preserve this kind of communal life in Santa Fe. The city fathers have had nothing to do with it, and there is a large and vociferous element that is ashamed of the town's informality. But it is lucky in possessing a population which is gregarious, and at the same time hostile to police regulation, and which remains loyal to a long-established tradition of group pleasures. Yet something of this color and vitality could be introduced to many other American cities; it is merely a matter of establishing (or re-establishing) the principle that streets are not intended solely for motor traffic but were made for any and every kind of outdoor group activity, from children's games to funeral processions and endless loitering in the sun. All civic architecture is essentially nothing but an appropriate background for this life; and city planning is chiefly justified when it helps preserve and foster informal communal activities.

As far as Santa Fe is concerned, we can be sure that the population will never entirely abandon even the widest and straightest of streets to motor traffic. There will always be some carefree jaywalker to cross in front of you without warning: a teenage motorcyclist to show off for the drugstore crowd: a dogfight or a wedding. Always, in short, a reminder that the motorist does not own the streets but merely shares them with others.

The Many Guises of Suburbia

ANYONE WHO HAS been around will have no trouble in im-
mediately recognizing this kind of community: It consists of
a hundred or more small dwellings, almost identical as to
size, construction, and plan, all apparently built at much the
same time. The community, located by itself in the midst of
farmland, appears to have been designed all of a piece: in
the layout of the streets and roads, in the siting of the
houses, in the central location of the public square there
are traces of an overall plan—usually a modified grid. Every
family in this community has pretty much the same income,
the same schooling, the same religious background, the
same way of life. Early in the morning the men go off to
work and leave the place to the women and children; they
come back tired late in the day. There are few if any jobs
in the community itself, and very little commercial life;
a trip from the house to get food is one of the chief diver-
sions of the women. Religious activities and women's organizations flourish, and so do men's organizations during their
free time. Considerable thought is given to correct and holiday attire, both by men and women. There is no cultural
life in the urban meaning of the term, but on the whole the
inhabitants seem to enjoy their routine existence. They do
not openly object to the pressures of convention and are
suspicious of eccentricity—particularly when it takes an
ostentatious form. Family life is made much of, and children
are early taught to respect the unwritten laws of the community. Outsiders visiting the place are usually appalled by
it; they wonder how anyone withstands the atmosphere of

[From *Landscape*, Vol. 11, No. 1, Autumn 1961]

conformity, and object that the community, for all its isolation, is not really country; for all its compactness, not really
urban. What they chiefly see and deplore is an overall uniformity—in architecture, in occupation, in routine, in dress
and manners.

If the reader has identified this community as being an
approximation of the average middle-class American suburb
or housing development he will have been correct; but he
will also have been correct if he identified it as a Southwestern Indian Pueblo or a Chinese farm village or an Italian
village like Silone's Fontamara or a farm community in
Eastern Europe or Asia or Latin America. Such communities
all differ as to economy, land tenure, geographical situation,
size and age, and degree of technical proficiency, but the way
of life is in many important respects the same in all of them.
Whatever the means of livelihood of their wage-earners—
office or factory work, work on a neighboring estate or on a
small plot of ground—these places appear to exist because
their inhabitants want neither the isolation of the open countryside nor the anonymity of the city; what they seem to
prefer is a small-scale society where happiness comes (or is
supposed to come) from conformity to a generally accepted
set of traditions and not from the pursuit of individual freedom. Nations older than we take this point of view more or
less for granted and even assume that it contributes to the
common good. Certainly few of them have examined the
tradition-minded community as closely and as critically as
we have examined our new suburbs. The absence of men
from most European farm villages during the daylight hours,
for instance, does not seem to have produced anything like
the abundance of psycho-sociological analysis that the same
situation has inspired in America.

Nevertheless it might be well if we ourselves studied some of those communities in order to find out a little how they have evolved, physically as well as socially, and what quality it is that they possess which enables them to multiply and endure. For it looks as if suburbs and a suburban way of life would be with us for a long time to come; and if we somehow learned to see them as belated American versions of an ancient and relatively effective world-wide community form instead of as land-speculation-induced nightmares we might adjust to them a little more gracefully and intelligently than we are doing now.

The Almost Perfect Town

"OPTIMO CITY (pop. 10,783, alt. 2100), situated on a small rise overlooking the N. branch of the Apache River, is a farm and ranch center served by a spur of the S.P. County seat of Sheridan Co., Optimo City (originally established in 1853 as Ft. Gaffney) was the scene of a bloody encounter with a party of marauding Indians in 1857. (See marker on courthouse lawn.) It is the location of a state Insane Asylum, of a sorghum processing plant and an overall factory. Annual County Fair and Cowboy Roundup Sept. 4. The highway now passes through a rolling countryside devoted to grain crops and cattle raising."

Thus would the state guide dispose of Optimo City and hasten on to a more spirited topic if Optimo City as such existed. Optimo City, however, is not one town, it is a hundred or more towns, all very much alike, scattered across the United States from the Alleghenies to the Pacific, most numerous west of the Mississippi and south of the Platte. When, for instance, you travel through Texas and Oklahoma and New Mexico and even parts of Kansas and Missouri, Optimo City is the blur of filling stations and motels you occasionally pass; the solitary traffic light, the glimpse up a side street of an elephantine courthouse surrounded by elms and sycamores, the brief congestion of mud-spattered pickup trucks that slows you down before you hit the open road once more. And fifty miles farther on Optimo City's identical twin appears on the horizon, and a half dozen more Optimos beyond that until at last, with some relief, you reach the metropolis

[From *Landscape*, Vol. 2, No. 1, Autumn 1952]

with its new housing developments and factories and the cluster of downtown skyscrapers.

Optimo City, then, is actually a very familiar feature of the American landscape. But since you have never stopped there except to buy gas, it might be well to know it a little better. What is there to see? Not a great deal, yet more than you would at first suspect.

Optimo, being after all an imaginary average small town, has to have had an average small-town history, or at least a Western version of that average. The original Fort Gaffney (named after some inconspicuous worthy in the U.S. Army) was really little more than a stockade on a bluff overlooking a ford in the river; a few roads or trails in the old days straggled out into the plain (or desert as they called it then), lost heart and disappeared two or three miles from town. Occasionally even today someone digs up a fragment of the palisade or a bit of rust-eaten hardware in the backyards of the houses near the center of town, and the historical society possesses what it claims is the key to the principal gate. But on the whole, Optimo City is not much interested in its martial past. The fort as a military installation ceased to exist during the Civil War, and the last of the pioneers died a half century ago before anyone had the historical sense to take down his story. And when the county seat was located in the town the name was changed from Fort Gaffney with its frontier connotation to Optimo, which means (so the townspeople will tell you) "I hope for the best" in Latin.

What Optimo is really proud of even now is its identity as county seat. Sheridan County (and you will do well to remember that it was NOT named after the notorious Union general but after Horace Sheridan, an early member of the territorial legislature; Optimo still feels strongly about what it calls the War between the States) was organized in the 1870's and there ensued a brief but lively competition for the possession of the courthouse between Optimo and the next largest settlement, Apache Center, twenty miles away. Optimo City won, and Apache Center, a cowtown with one paved street, is not allowed to forget the fact. The football and basketball games between the Optimo Cougars and the Apache Braves are still characterized by a very special sort of rivalry. No matter how badly beaten Optimo City often is, it consoles itself by remembering that it is still the county seat, and that Apache Center, in spite of the brute cunning of its team, has still only one street paved. We shall presently come back to the meaning of that boast.

To get on with the history of Optimo.

The Inflexible Gridiron

Aided by the state and Army engineers, the city fathers, back in the seventies, surveyed and laid out the new metropolis. As a matter of course they located a square or public place in the center of the town and eventually they built their courthouse in the middle of the square; such having been the layout of every county seat these Western Americans had ever seen. Streets led from the center of each side of the square, being named Main Street North and South, and Sheridan Street East and West. Eventually these four streets and the square were surrounded by a gridiron pattern of streets and avenues—all numbered or lettered, and all of them totally oblivious of the topography of the town. Some streets charge up impossibly steep slopes, straight as an arrow; others lead off into the tangle of alders and cottonwoods near the river and get lost.

Strangely enough, this inflexibility in the plan has had some very pleasant results. South Main Street, which leads from the square down to the river, was too steep in the old days for heavily laden wagons to climb in wet weather, so at the foot of it on the flats near the river, those merchants who dealt in farm produce and farm equipment built their stores and warehouses. The blacksmith and welder, the hay and grain supply, and finally the auction ring and the farmers' market found South Main the best location in town for their purpose—which purpose being primarily dealing with out-of-town farmers and ranchers. And when, after considerable pressure on the legislature and much resistance from Apache Center (which already had a railroad) the Southern Pacific built a spur to Optimo, the depot was naturally built at the foot of South Main. And of course the grain elevator and the stockyards were built near the railroad. The railroad spur was intended to make Optimo into a manufacturing city, and never did; all that ever came was a small overall factory and a plant for processing sorghum with a combined payroll of about 150. Most of the workers in the two establishments are Mexicans from south of the border—locally referred to in polite circles as "Latinos" or "Hispanos." They have built for themselves flimsy little houses under the cottonwoods and next to the river. "If ever we have an epidemic in Optimo," the men at the courthouse remark, "it will break out first of all in those Latino shacks." But they have done nothing as yet about providing them with better houses, and probably never will.

Downtown and Uptown

Depot, market, factories, warehouses, slum—these features, combined with the fascination of the river bank and

stockyards and the assorted public of railroaders and Latinos
and occasional ranch hands—have all given South Main a very
definite character: easy-going, loud, colorful, and perhaps
during fair week or at shipping time a little disreputable.
Boys on the Cougar football squad have specific orders to
stay away from South Main, but they don't. Actually the
whole of Optimo looks on the section with indulgence and
pride; it makes the townspeople feel that they understand
metropolitan problems when they can compare South Main
with the New York waterfront.

North Main, up on the heights beyond the Courthouse
Square and past the two or three blocks of retail stores, is
(on the other hand) the very finest part of Optimo. The
northwestern section of town, with its tree-shaded streets,
its view over the river and the prairie, its summer breezes,
has always been identified with wealth and fashion as Optimo
understands them. Colonel Ephraim Powell (Confederate
Army, Ret., owner of some of the best ranch country in the
region) built his bride a handsome limestone house with a
slate roof and a tower, and Walter Slymaker, proprietor of
Slymaker's Mercantile and of the grain elevator, not to be
outdone, built an even larger house farther up Main; so did
Hooperson, first president of the bank. There are a dozen
such houses in all, stone or Milwaukee brick with piazzas (or
galleries, as the old timers still call them) and large, untidy
gardens around them. It is worth noting, by the way, that
the brightest claim to aristocratic heritage is this: grandfather
came out West for his health. New England may have its
"Mayflower" and "Arabella," East Texas its Three Hundred Founding Families, New Mexico its Conquistadores;
but Optimo is loyal to the image of the delicate young college
graduate who arrived by train with his law books, his set of

Dickens, his taste for wine, and the custom of dressing for
dinner. This legendary figure has about seen his day in the
small talk of Optimo society, and the younger generation
frankly doubts his having ever existed; but he (or his ghost)
had a definite effect on local manners and ways of living. At
all events, because of this memory Optimo looks down on
those Western mining towns where Sarah Bernhardt and de
Reszke and Oscar Wilde seem to have played so many one-
night stands in now-vanished opera houses.

A World in Itself

Wickedness—or the suggestion of wickedness—at one end
of Main, affluence and respectability at the other. How about
Sheridan Street running East and West? That is where you'll
find most of the stores; in the first four or five blocks on
either side of the Courthouse Square. They form a rampart;
narrow brick houses, most of them two stories high with
elaborate cornices and long narrow windows; all of them de-
void of modern commercial graces of chromium and black
glass and artful window display, all of them ugly but all of
them pretty uniform; and so you have on Sheridan Street
something rarely seen in urban America: a harmonious and
restful and dignified business section. Only eight or ten
blocks of it in all, to be sure; turn any corner and you are at
once in a residential area.

Here there is block after block of one-story frame houses
with trees in front and picket fences or hedges; no sidewalk after the first block or so; a hideous church (without
a cemetery of course); a small-time auto repair shop in
someone's back yard; dirt roadway; and if you follow the
road a few blocks more—say to 10th Street (after that there

are no more signs) you are likely to see a tractor turn into someone's drive with wisps of freshly-cut alfalfa clinging to the vertical sickle bar. The countryside is that close to the heart of Optimo City, farmers are that much part of the town. And the glimpse of the tractor (like the glimpse of a deer or a fox driven out of the hills by a heavy winter) restores for a moment a feeling for an old kinship that seemed to have been destroyed forever. But this is what makes Optimo, the hundreds of Optimos throughout America, so valuable; the ties between country and town have not yet been broken. Limited though it may well be in many ways, the world of Optimo City is still complete.

The center of this world is Courthouse Square, with the courthouse, ponderous, barbaric, and imposing, in the center of that. The building and its woebegone little park not only interrupts the vistas of Main and Sheridan—it was intended to do this—it also interrupts the flow of traffic in all four directions. A sluggish eddy of vehicles and pedestrians is the result, Optimo's animate existence slowed and intensified. The houses on the four sides of the square are of the same vintage (and the same general architecture) as the monument in their midst: mid-nineteenth-century brick or stone; cornices like the brims of hats, fancy dripstones over the arched windows like eyebrows; painted blood-red or mustard-yellow or white; identical except for the six-story Gaffney Hotel and the classicism of the First National Bank.

Every house has a tin roof porch extending over the sidewalk, a sort of permanent awning which protects passersby and incidentally conceals the motley of store windows and signs. To walk around the square and down Sheridan Street under a succession of these galleries or metal awnings, crossing the strips of bright sunlight between the roofs of different

height, is one of the delights of Optimo—one of its amenities
in the English use of that word. You begin to understand
why the Courthouse Square is such a popular part of town.

Saturday Nights—Bright Lights

Saturday, of course, is the best day for seeing the full tide
of human existence in Sheridan County. The rows of parked
pickups are like cattle in a feed lot; the sidewalks in front
of Slymaker's Mercantile, the Ranch Cafe, Sears, the drugstore, resound to the mincing steps of cowboy boots; farmers
and ranchers, thumbs in their pants pockets, gather in groups
to lament the drought (there is always a drought) and those
men in Washington, while their wives go from store to movie
house to store. Radios, jukeboxes, the bell in the courthouse
tower; the teenagers doing "shave-and-a-haircut; bay rum"
on the horns of their parents' cars as they drive round and
round the square. The smell of hot coffee, beer, popcorn,
exhaust, alfafa, cow manure. A man is trying to sell a truckload of grapefruit so that he can buy a truckload of cinder-
blocks to sell somewhere else. Dogs; ten-year-old cowboys
firing cap pistols at each other. The air is full of pigeons,
floating candy wrappers, the flat strong accent erroneously
called Texan.

All these people are here in the center of Optimo for many
reasons—for sociability first of all, for news, for the spending
and making of money, for relaxation. "Jim Guthrie and wife
were in town last week, visiting friends and transacting business," is the way the Sheridan *Sentinel* describes it; and
almost all of Jim Guthrie's business takes place in the
square. That is one of the peculiarities of Optimo and one
of the reasons why the square as an institution is so impor-

tant. For it is around the square that the oldest and most
essential urban (or county) services are established. Here
are the firms under local control and ownership, those devoted
almost exclusively to the interest of the surrounding countryside. Upstairs are the lawyers, doctors, dentists, insurance
firms, the public stenographer, the Farm Bureau. Downstairs
are the bank, the prescription drugstore, the newspaper
office, and of course Slymaker's Mercantile and the Ranch
Cafe.

Influence of the Courthouse

Why have the chain stores not invaded this part of town in
greater force? Some have already got a foothold, but most
of them are at the far end of Sheridan or even out on the
Federal Highway. The presence of the courthouse is partly
responsible. The traditional services want to be as near the
courthouse as they can, and real-estate values are high. The
courthouse itself attracts so many out-of-town visitors that
the problem of parking is acute. The only solution that occurs to the enlightened minds of the Chamber of Commerce
is to tear the courthouse down, use the place for parking,
and build a new one somewhere else. They have already had
an architect draw a sketch of a new courthouse to go at the
far end of Main Street; a chaste concrete cube with vertical
motifs between the windows—a fine specimen of bureaucrat
modernism. But the trouble is, where to get the money for
a new courthouse when the old one is still quite evidently
adequate and in constant use?

   If you enter the courthouse you will be amazed by two
things: the horrifying architecture of the place, and the variety of functions it fills. Courthouse means of course court-

rooms, and there are two of those. Then there is the office
of the County Treasurer, the Road Commissioner, the School
Board, the Agricultural Agent, the Extension Agent, Sanitary
Inspector, and usually a group of Federal agencies as well—
PMA, Soil Conservation, FHA and so on. Finally the Red
Cross, the Boy Scouts, and the District Nurse. No doubt
many of these offices are tiresome examples of government
interference in private matters; just the same, they are for
better or worse part of almost every farmer's and rancher's
business, and the courthouse, in spite of all the talk about
county consolidation, is a more important place than ever.

As it is, the ugly old building has conferred upon Optimo
a blessing which many larger and richer American towns can
envy: a center for civic activity and a symbol for civic pride
—something as different from the modern "civic center"
as day is from night. Contrast the array of classic edifices,
lost in the midst of waste space, the meaningless pomp of
flag poles and war memorials and dribbling fountains of any
American city from San Francisco to Washington with the
animation and harmony and the almost domestic intimacy
of Optimo Courthouse Square, and you have a pretty good
measure of what is wrong with much American city planning; civic consciousness has been divorced from everyday
life, put in a special zone all by itself. Optimo City has its
zones; but they are organically related to one another.

Doubtless the time will never come that the square is
studied as a work of art. Why should it be? The craftsman-
ship in the details, the architecture of the building, the notions of urbanism in the layout of the square itself are all
on a very countrified level. Still, such a square as this has
dignity and even charm. The charm is perhaps antiquarian
—a bit of rural America of seventy-five years ago; the dignity

is something else again. It derives from the function of the courthouse and the square, and from its peculiarly national character.

Communal Center

The practice of erecting a public building in the center of an open place is in fact pretty well confined to America—more specifically to nineteenth-century America. The vast open areas favored by eighteenth-century European planners were usually kept free of construction, and public buildings—churches and palaces and law-courts—were located to face these squares; to command them, as it were. But they were not allowed to interfere with the original open effect. Even the plans of eighteenth-century American cities, such as Philadelphia and Reading and Savannah and Washington, always left the square or public place intact. Spanish America, of course, provides the best illustrations of all; the plaza, nine times out of ten, is surrounded by public buildings, but it is left free. Yet almost every American town laid out after (say) 1820 deliberately planted a public building in the center of its square. Sometimes it was a school, sometimes a city hall, more often a courthouse, and it was always approachable from all four sides and always as conspicuous as possible.

Why? Why did these pioneer city fathers go counter to the taste of the past in this matter? One guess is as good as another. Perhaps they were so proud of their representative institutions that they wanted to give their public buildings the best location available. Perhaps frontier America was following an aesthetic movement, already at that date strong in Europe, that held that an open space was improved when it contained some prominent free-standing object—an obelisk or a statue or a triumphal arch. However that may have been, the pioneer Americans went Europe one better, and put the largest building in town right in the center of the square.

Thus the square ceased to be thought of in nineteenth-century America as a vacant space; it became a container or (if you prefer) a frame. A frame, so it happened, not merely for the courthouse, but for all activity of a communal sort. Few aesthetic experiments have ever produced such brilliantly practical results. A society which had long since ceased to rally around the individual leader and his residence and which was rapidly tiring of rallying around the meeting-house or church all at once found a new symbol: local representative government, or the courthouse. A good deal of flagwaving resulted—as European travelers have always told us—and a good deal of very poor "representational" architecture; but Optimo acquired something to be proud of, something to moderate that American tendency to think of every town as existing entirely for money-making purposes.

Symbol of Independence

At this juncture the protesting voice of the Chamber of Commerce is heard. "One moment. Before you finish with our courthouse you had better hear the other side of the question. If the courthouse were torn down we would not only have more parking space—sorely needed in Optimo—we would also get funds for widening Main Street into a four-lane highway. If Main Street were widened Optimo could attract many new businesses catering to tourists and other transients—restaurants and motels and garages and all sorts of drive-in establishments. In the last ten years" (continues

the Chamber of Commerce) "Optimo has grown by twelve
hundred. *Twelve hundred!* At that rate we'll still be a small
town of less than twenty thousand in 1999. But if we had
new businesses we'd grow fast and have better schools and
a new hospital, and the young people wouldn't move to
the cities. Or do you expect Optimo to go on depending on
a few hundred tight-fisted farmers and ranchers for its
livelihood?" The voice, now shaking with emotion, adds
something about "eliminating" South Main by means of
an embankment and a clover leaf and picnic grounds for
tourists under the cottonwoods where the Latinos still reside.

These suggestions are very sensible ones on the whole.
Translate them into more general terms and what they
amount to is this: if we want to get ahead, the best thing to
do is break with our own past, become as independent as
possible of our *immediate* environment and at the same time
become almost completely dependent for our well-being on
some remote outside resource. Whatever you may think of
such a program, you cannot very well deny that it has been
successful for a large number of American towns. Think of
the hayseed communities which have suddenly found themselves next to an oil field or a large factory or an Army installation, and which have cashed in on their good fortune
by transforming themselves overnight, turning their backs
on their former sources of income, and tripling their population in a few years! It is true that these towns put all their
eggs in one basket, that they are totally at the mercy of some
large enterprise quite beyond their control. But think of the
freedom from local environment; think of the excitement
and the money! Given the same circumstances—and the
Southwest is full of surprises still—why should Optimo not
do the same?

A Common Destiny

Because there are many different kinds of towns just as there
are many different kinds of men; a development which is
good for one kind can be death on another. Apache Center
(to use that abject community as an example), with its stockyards and its one paved street and its very limited responsibility to the county, as a community might well become a
boom-town and no one would be worse off. Optimo seems
to have a different destiny. For almost a hundred years—a
long time in this part of the world—it has been identified
with the surrounding landscape and been an essential part
of it. Whatever wealth it possesses has come from the farms
and ranches, not from the overall factory or from tourists.
The bankers and merchants will tell you, of course, that without their ceaseless efforts and their vision the countryside
could never have existed; the farmers and ranchers consider
Optimo's prosperity and importance entirely their own creation. Both parties are right to the extent that the town is part
of the landscape—one might even say part of every farm,
since much farm business takes place in the town itself.

Now if Optimo suddenly became a year-round tourist
resort, or the overall capital of the Southwest; what would
happen to that relationship, do you suppose? It would
vanish. The farmers and ranchers would soon find themselves
crowded out, and would go elsewhere for those services and
benefits which they now enjoy in Optimo. And as for Optimo itself, it would soon achieve the flow of traffic, the new
store fronts, the housing developments, the payrolls and
bank accounts it cannot help dreaming about; and in the
same process achieve a total social and physical dislocation,
and a loss of a sense of its own identity. County Seat of

Sheridan County? Yes; but much more important: Southwestern branch of the "American Cloak and Garment Cor-
poration"; or the LITTLE TOWN WITH THE BIG WELCOME—300
tourist beds which, when empty for one night out of three,
threaten bankruptcy to half the town.

As of the present, Optimo remains pretty much as it has
been for the last generation. The Federal Highway still by-
passes the center (what a roadblock, symbolical as well as
actual, that Courthouse is!); so if you want to see Optimo,
you had better turn off at the top of the hill near the water-
tower of the lunatic asylum—now called Fairview State Rest
Home, and with the hideous high fence around it torn down.
The dirt road eventually becomes North Main. The old
Slymaker place is still intact. The Powell mansion, galleries
and all, belongs to the American Legion, and a funeral home
has taken over the Hooperson house. Then comes downtown
Optimo; and then the Courthouse, huge and graceless, in
detail and proportion more like a monstrous birdhouse than
a monument. Stop here. You'll find nothing of interest in
the stores, and no architectural gems down a side street.
Even if there were, no one would be able to point them out.
The historical society, largely in the hands of ladies, thinks
of antiquity in terms of antiques, and art as anything that
looks pretty on the mantelpiece.

The weather is likely to be scorching hot and dry, with
a wild ineffectual breeze in the elms and sycamores. You'll
find no restaurant in town with atmosphere—no chandeliers
made out of wagon wheels, no wall decorations of famous
brands, no bar disguised as the Hitching Rail or the Old
Corral. Under a high ceiling with a two-bladed fan in the
middle, you'll eat ham hock and beans, hot bread, iced tea

without lemon, and like it or go without. But as compensation of sorts at the next table there will be two ranchers eating with their hats on, and discussing the affairs, public and private, of Optimo City. To hear them talk, you'd think they owned the town.

That's about all. There's the market at the foot of South Main, the Latino shacks around the overall factory, a grove of cottonwoods, and the Apache River (North Branch) trickling down a bed ten times too big; and then the open country. You may be glad to have left Optimo behind.

Or you may have liked it, and found it pleasantly old-fashioned. Perhaps it is; but it is in no danger of dying out quite yet. As we said to begin with, there is another Optimo City fifty miles farther on. The country is covered with them. Indeed they are so numerous that it sometimes seems as if Optimo and rural America were one and indivisible.

To Pity the Plumage and Forget the Dying Bird

WE LIKE TO THINK of ourselves as an urban people, but much depends on what we mean by urban. The National Planning Association informs us that by 1975, seventy-three per cent of the American population will be living in metropolitan areas. A very impressive statistic until we discover that among these metropolitan areas are Pittsfield, Massachusetts, Waterloo, Iowa, and Laredo, Texas, with a projected population of 88,000.

At present, fifty-eight per cent of our population lives in towns of 50,000 or less; more Americans live in towns of 10,000 or less than live in all of the cities of a million or more; and one out of every four Americans lives in a place with less than 2,500 inhabitants. Most of us, in brief, still live in a small city or in a semi-rural setting, and the chances are that even in 1975 the proportion will still be sizeable.

One puzzling thing about this situation is, who is responsible for the rural, small-town, small-city environment: county? state? Federal government? What group, what profession, what department is primarily concerned with its well-being? Now that the cities have their own Department of Housing and Urban Development they cannot complain of neglect; forests and public lands are taken care of by the Department of the Interior; the Corps of Engineers and the various state highway commissions have their own bailiwicks. But who is responsible for what is left of the American landscape? Who is interested in making it more livable?

More livable, not necessarily more beautiful. Scenically speaking, few parts of the world can boast of such magnifi-

[From *Landscape*, Vol. 17, No. 1, Autumn 1967]

cent countryside or such attractive towns as those in the
United States. A tight fitting together of all the parts, a
crowded efficiency is not so typical of this country as it is of
older landscapes, and the architecture and monuments in our
towns are not usually worth a second glance. But nowhere
else are the works of man on such a generous scale, nowhere
else do towns and cities stand out so dramatically against
their setting. There are hundreds of towns with long straight
streets engulfed in shade trees, hundreds of suburbs that are
models for the rest of the Western world; charming cam-
puses unique to America, and more often than not an old-
fashioned urban dignity achieved with the simplest of means.
Nowhere are newly built towns so bright and full of energy;
even the ugliest of main streets is enlivened by the occasional
elegance of a shopping center, a cluster of grain elevators,
a burst of greenery. The towns and small cities of Europe
are fast being submerged by a flood of good taste; theirs is
the fixed smile of welcome to tourists; over here we still
retain a varied and exuberant beauty. It is impossible after
traveling through the American landscape from city to town
to village, not to feel love for it, and finally a pride of possession.

But it is then that you begin to see the landscape with a
different eye and to see what you had not seen before.

You turn off the broad highway, leaving the panoramas behind, and follow a dirt road that humps straight ahead out
of sight; no roadside landscaping here, merely a borrow pit
deep enough to drown in; but the road seems little used.
There is a grey, dilapidated house with a swarm of junked
cars under the half dead trees of the orchard. The barn is
about to fall down, erosion is eating into the cornfield. Half

a mile ahead is a crossroad (this one all but abandoned) with
another decrepit house, a weed-grown cemetery, and a vacant
church. There is a third house with a half dozen trailers in
the front yard. The place is littered with trash and broken
toys.

The road, now grass-grown, follows a stream through a
disorderly tangle of vines and trees, and you see how the
water is dirtied by the overflow from a nearby feedlot. Eventually it leads to a lake, the lower end of which has been
transformed into a swamp by the enormous steep embankment of a new highway. The dirt road falters, looks for its
path among stumps and puddles, and finally goes through an
underpass.

Ten minutes later you succeed in getting onto the new
divided, limited access highway. It cuts diagonally across
the pattern of fields and roads and fences so that the right
of way has a kind of sawtooth border of triangular pieces of
land. Each sprouts a sign: FOR SALE, WILL FILL (or LEVEL) TO
SUIT TENANT, INDUSTRIAL SITE. The nearer you get to town
the thicker the signs and billboards become, then service
stations, trailer courts, used-car lots, supermarkets, and
motels appear. On dirt roads bulldozed through alfalfa fields
stand rows of identical tract houses, all perched on fill held
in place by a scanty growth of grass. The climax to the
whole strip development is "Towne and Country Plaza,"
a stylish 300,000 square foot shopping center recently built
by a Chicago firm, and almost entirely tenanted by chain
stores.

Town itself, as approached by the new highway, has a
familiar aspect: a mass of trees, a steeple or two, one tall
conspicuous building. The water tower is adorned with spray-
can inscriptions of high school scores. As usual, Main Street

is wide and handsome, with splendid maple trees in the
residential section, solid white houses each with an immaculate lawn. The side streets display the same formal beauty,
though on a smaller scale.

Getting through the business district is no easy under-
taking since it has been transformed, from motives of efficiency, into a maze of one-way streets. But there are solid
brick churches, solid banks which tell both the temperature
and the time, and several blocks of not so solid looking retail stores, some of them for rent. In an effort to promote a
festive downtown atmosphere, plastic geraniums have been
hung from the light poles. In the basement of the yellow
brick hotel is the office of the Chamber of Commerce: BLANK
TOWN, THE DASH CAPITAL OF THE WORLD. THE FRIENDLY TOWN
WITH A BIG FUTURE. VISIT THE WORLD FAMOUS MYSTERY ROCKS.
INDUSTRIAL SITES AVAILABLE.

All of this constitutes the conventional transient view of the
town; what every tourist sees and usually likes; it is very
reassuring: America is the best country in the world. But
when you deliberately turn off Main Street and head for the
station in the lower part of town you see something different.
Cross Third Street and Second Street and Railroad Street;
the buildings are shabby, the stick-style depot is boarded up.
The surface of the streets is broken and full of dusty holes;
there are overhead lines and half the trees are dying. Instead
of neat white houses as in the upper section there are close
packed rows of frame tenements and duplexes dating from
1893, an occasional vacant lot, garages black with grease,
corner groceries with screen doors, lodging houses. Here is
where the local minority lives: Negroes or Spanish Americans or Indians or unassimilated Hillbillies along with idle

old men and drifters vaguely looking for a harvesting or construction job. The section merges into a wasteland of rusting tracks, cinders, flood plain. Most of the people here are on relief, but some work in the nearby factory.

It makes wire coat-hangers or carburetors for power lawn mowers or plastic bookends; whatever it makes, the byproduct is a black fluid which oozes down the margin of McKinley Avenue, passes through a used car lot, under some billboards until it spills into the river. The billboards say KEEP ILLINOIS (or ALABAMA or COLORADO) BEAUTIFUL; BUY A FORD; SUPPORT YOUR LOCAL POLICE.

There is a fine municipal swimming pool, a fine football field, a country club with a golf course, a county fair grounds in poor shape. Fairmonte Acres is the choice suburb; it has gas lighting along its winding roads named after Indian tribes.

The street leading out of town passes several trailer courts, not very pretty ones, then it rejoins the highway; once more you are in the midst of well-cared-for fields, winding valleys full of greenery; and off on the horizon, fifteen miles away, is another water tower, and presumably another town like the one behind you.

What does a detour of this sort reveal? Nothing deliberately hidden, merely that much of the American landscape, even in prosperous areas, is neglected and mismanaged, constricted by long out of date ideas of planning and preservation.

It reveals that widespread reform and change are in order; but what kind of reform? There is a sharp difference of opinion here as to whether it should be ecological or social. The so-called beautificationists, together with the many groups and foundations dedicated to quality in the environ-

ment, and some of the old-line landscape architects and
regional planners are chiefly worried about preserving and
improving the natural features of the environment—*any*
environment—and for several reasons theirs are the voices
we hear most often. In the case of this particular landscape
they have a set of ready answers: "Hide the junked cars,
turn the stream into a recreation area, turn the road into a
bridle path or bicycle path, the eroded fields into a forest or
a nature study preserve. As for the town itself, the former
nineteenth-century appearance of Main Street should be
carefully restored, more trees planted and the factory told
not to pollute the river. The billboards, the trailer courts and
all other aspects of urban sprawl should be eliminated, and
tourists should be attracted by means of an 'Annual Pioneer
Pageant.' Would it be possible" (a diffident tone creeps
into their voices) "to revive handicrafts? Bedspreads and
homemade jam?"

Well, no; but otherwise these proposals are sensible enough.
If they were put into effect the landscape would undoubtedly be more sightly, and in ecological terms, much more
healthy. Health and recreation—they have become almost
obsessions with some environmental reformers; are they
the only things that matter?

There exists, however, another way of approaching the
neglected and mismanaged landscape, and this other way is
just as much concerned with the people who live there as
with the countryside or town itself. Health and recreation
are essential to the people, of course, but no less essential
are the possibilities of making a good living and of being
active members of society. Who belongs to this other school?
Some are rural sociologists, some are government officials—
Agriculture, oeo, Welfare. Others are the latter day home-

steaders, like those the "Green Revolution" and "Way Out" describe; advocates of "intentional communities," refugees from the metropolis. Then there are members of farm reform movements, decentralists, rural priests and school teachers. Very few come from the design professions. What they all seem to have in common is a desire to see rural small-city America revitalized socially and economically, and they are all trying to do something to bring this to pass.

This second group of reformers sees the problems in a light entirely different from that of the ecologically minded. To them this landscape—well above the American average in livability, or health for that matter—is suffering from a very specific ailment or combination of ailments: poverty and political inertia. These can eventually ruin the most fertile countrysides in the richest among nations; likewise prosperity and modernization can restore them and in the process restore their beauty.

The reactions of the two groups to public eyesores— especially junked cars and trailers—are typical. The beautificationists view them quite simply as deliberate affronts to the passerby, expressions of total indifference to questions of taste. In a sense they are not so wrong. But by this time everyone ought to know that junked cars in a farmyard or a pasture have an economic explanation: they mean poverty. Poverty *and* laziness, or poverty *and* ignorance; but poverty in any case. Junked cars are where they are either to be cannibalized to produce one half-way decent car for a family which cannot afford to buy one, or else because a city junk dealer is paying a small rent in order to park his surplus stock.

The same holds true of many billboards: they represent

a small income to an impoverished landowner. It is very
convenient to ascribe the despoliation of our landscape to
the greed of large economic interests: power companies, coal
mining companies, lumber companies, ranchers and real
estate developers with immense land holdings. All these
certainly contribute to the mess, and they are the ones
who especially threaten exurbia where most of the Beautificationists live. So the cry goes up that if we once teach
social responsibility to capitalism, all will be saved. But who
is going to teach social responsibility to the poor? The
sad truth of the matter is that most of the damage is done
by them. Much strip mining is the work of unemployed
miners who happen to own a few acres of coal-rich land.
Much overgrazing and indiscriminate tree cutting is the work
of needy farmers and stockmen; water is polluted by families
which have no decent plumbing, by small, inefficient country
operators; and a 1956 jalopy is more likely to pollute the air
than a 1969 Cadillac. For every poorly designed, poorly located
subdivision owned by a multi-million-dollar developer, there
are a dozen small ones, no less poorly designed, owned by
a farmer short of cash or sick of being poor. The moment
we get the courage to blame poverty for some of our environmental troubles we will have taken the first real step
to reform.

If the Soil Conservation Service is right, there are about
300,000 miles of streambank in the United States that are
not covered by any conservation program. Most of this is
in private hands, and the average farmer or rancher does not
have the money to undertake reclaiming or reseeding land
at $300 an acre. So he continues to abuse the stream, even
though it is of no value to him. Is there really any sense in
preaching a "new land ethic" to men who would promptly

wind up on relief if they practiced it? Poverty, as the French
say, is not a vice. Perhaps not, but it is a bad habit which
interferes with good habits.

Poverty in the country, smelling of laying mash and kerosene.
Poverty, public or corporate, in the towns and small cities
manifest in slums, pollution, unpaved streets and a deter-
mination not to change. Perhaps what our smaller munici-
palities need is a guaranteed annual income: pressed by the
constant cry for new streets, new schools, by higher welfare
costs, the only solution they see is to attract more industry.
And when they *do* manage to attract a plant the last thing
they dream of doing is protecting the air and water from
pollution. What available money there is either goes into
trying to keep downtown alive, or into the inevitable youth
facilities—athletic fields, schools, recreation programs. What
you find in small American factory or mining towns, and
even in farm processing towns in Kansas or Texas are not
the most extensive slums, but far too often the *worst* slums:
dirtier, more primitive, more ghetto-like, more isolated from
the rest of the community than any slum in Chicago or New
York. The proportion of substandard housing in rural America is four times what it is in the cities, and though this includes the shanties of the cotton South, the shacks, tents,
chicken coops, and car bodies where some 60,000 Southwestern Indians live, it also includes the squalid trailer courts,
the miserable do-it-yourself houses along unpaved streets
on the edge of town, the company tenements which no large
city would tolerate, if only for health reasons. The trailer
and the trailer court are for hundreds of thousands of Americans the only alternative to slum living. But they have another virtue: along with the new highway they disrupt the

old pattern of the city and destroy established land values,
and thus represent real possibilities of change.

As the OEO has discovered, poverty is not an easy thing to
define, particularly in a landscape of million dollar farms,
million dollar schools, multimillion dollar highways and
space age industries with their attendant $30,000 suburban
homes. But we are learning not to confuse these installations
with those which contribute to the permanent well-being of
the landscape and its inhabitants. They can and often do
exist in the midst of an environment which in human terms
suffers from severe impoverishment.

An impoverished environment is one which can no longer
help the people who live in it to become full-fledged individuals and citizens. Not all of our development comes
from contact with the environment; but much of it does, and
when that contact is made difficult we are badly cheated.
Each of us needs a chance to create or modify some part of
our world—house or place of work or place of leisure; and
an environment which is so mismanaged and disorganized
that most of us are simply tenants or guests or spectators can
be called impoverished. That is what has happened in many
parts of America. The young American without means can
sooner hope to be president of a bank than the owner of a
working farm; there are millions who can never aspire to
owning a house. More than one European country is actively
encouraging some form of ownership of land—if no more
than a vacation cottage or a garden plot. We have pretty well
outgrown the nineteenth-century concept of the homestead
and the family farm; but there are other forms of land tenure that we have yet to try. The real-estate developer, whatever his ethical shortcomings, has broken the inflexible pattern

of one kind of ownership. The highway, on the other hand, threatens to become the landscape of franchises—an area all but inaccessible to the small operator. Our countryside can become the same thing unless we pay attention. How many of our states and counties are thinking about new, more flexible, more equitable forms of land tenure?

An environment is impoverished when its internal structure is too rigid to change on its own—and when the public authorities make no real effort to change it to suit new circumstances. We are seeing land holdings getting larger and more specialized, new kinds of farm centers evolving, old centers going out of existence, and all of these developments call for new political forms and new types of administrative units. But our countryside remains entangled in a web of inefficient, arbitrary boundary lines which handicap social or economic action: obsolete townships and counties and school districts, expensive to operate; property lines based on the old grid system which paid no attention to topography; administrative frontiers which correspond to no social entity. How many enterprises, how many promising centers has this system not already strangled? But how many of our states and counties are giving serious thought to some kind of territorial and administrative reorganization? In the last twenty-five years *eight* counties out of the thousands in existence have been consolidated.

An environment is impoverished when its inhabitants cannot come together easily and agreeably, and when there are no suitable places of public assembly. Much of our rural road network, based as it is on the old-fashioned grid, is hopelessly inadequate, costly in maintenance, little used. Larger farms mean that many farmsteads are now remote

from adequate roads; faster forms of transportation mean
that farmers are abandoning old centers in favor of newer,
more distant ones. Yet the old network persists, leading
straight to places no one wants to go to any more. Fewer but
better and more direct highways are what the countryside
calls for. And in the towns and cities it is much the same.
There are still a disgraceful number of unpaved streets, based
as usual on a grid system which has at present no justification
—menaces to health, eyesores, social stigmas, and obstacles
to public assembly. Political inertia and lack of imagina-
tion are again to blame: we continue to perpetuate a street
system which focusses on the old downtown business
section and local traffic, instead of on the new recreation
and shopping centers where people would prefer to go. Main
Street is no longer the civic center, it is no longer the place
where citizen decisions are reached, if for no other reason
than that it no longer has parking space. How many of our
states and counties and smaller cities are seriously studying
the need for a rational road and street system which would
serve the new centers of activity?

Finally, an environment which has no conscious purpose,
which is incapable of deciding its own future, which does
not know how to locate highways, developments, industries,
recreation areas, new areas for exploitation except on a hit
or miss basis, is robbing its inhabitants of any kind of economic security and making responsible citizenship next to
impossible. How many of our states and counties have a
comprehensive plan for land use and future growth?

Economic poverty and political inertia are certainly not confined to the rural small-city countryside in America, but here
they are a peculiar kind of menace, because they are well

disguised. Yet no matter how beautiful our landscapes may appear to be, they are often inadequate as settings for a well-rounded life. The divisions of land, down to the smallest farm, and its tenure are frequently neither just nor efficient; the coming together of people for business or public affairs is unnecessarily handicapped; the destruction of symbols and monuments continues; and the need for a new public landscape of new boundaries, new roads, new centers, rededicated sites is still not taken seriously.

The question comes up again: who is going to devote time and energy to the helping of this neglected landscape? If we are at last trying to do something to make our cities more livable we can thank the sociologists and planners and economists and political scientists who have shown us what was wrong. The problems of this other America are very similar, but they call for a different approach; we are dealing here with a different kind of economy, a different kind of society, and a different kind of environment. It would be encouraging to believe that the environmental designers, particularly the landscape architects, could in time direct this particular war against poverty. There is a long and valuable tradition in landscape architecture of involvement in the total rural small-city landscape, dating back in this country more than a century to Andrew Jackson Downing, and reinvigorated two generations ago by L. H. Bailey: wilderness, park, and suburb to those men and their followers were little more than specialized fields in the wider province of landscape architecture, and they would have had little patience with the current exclusive enthusiasm for recreation areas. What seems to have happened is that a generation of environmental designers has allowed itself to be persuaded by the beautificationists and their ample financial resources that the task

of preserving Marin County, California, or Westchester
County, New York, is somehow worthier of its talents than
is the preservation of Madison County, Arkansas, or
Cheyenne County, Nebraska.

How long is this illusion likely to last? First of all, until
the environmental design pr fessions take one look at Cheyenne County and *see* what ails it. But what is also essential
is for every reponsible American to add a new social dimension to his definition of landscape beauty. We will have to
see that an inhabited landscape is neither beautiful nor sound
unless it makes possible an unfolding of the individual in
work and social relationships just as much as in health and
recreation.

"We are dealing with a problem more complex than billboards and automobile junkyards, utility poles and telephone wires," W. A. Crook declared at the 1965 Texas Conference on Our Environmental Crisis.*

"The crisis is one of human worth. Planting hedges around
junkyards, banning billboards from roadsides and going
underground with telephone lines will have cosmetic effects,
but the nation is not just disheveled, it is sick, and it needs
medicine as well as cosmetics. . . . Unless the attempts to
beautify our physical environment are coordinated with even
more serious efforts to meet the gut needs of society, they will
prove more detrimental than helpful. They will prevent diag-
nosis and treatment."

* "Poverty and the Obstinate Urge to Beauty," *Texas Conference on
Our Environmental Crisis* (Austin: School of Architecture, University
of Texas, 1966), p. 37.

The Social Landscape

OUR RELATIONSHIP WITH the environment, natural and man-made, has greatly changed in the past fifty years. We used to believe that a truly harmonious relationship would result when man took his identity from his setting. Environmentalism, under one name or another, was a popular doctrine: we were all products of our environment, and so the design and care of the environment was of great importance. Now we have begun to search for identity in other ways; and more and more we are inclined to manipulate the environment, use it as a tool for creating our identity.

The search for identity assumes many forms; one which directly affects the landscape is a growing dependence on other people, a gregariousness. What we are (or think we are) is not simply a matter of what we do and accomplish, but of how we affect others. Just as we say there is no sound unless there is an ear to register it, we also assume that there is no human identity unless there is another person to recognize it. We seem to be redefining man once again as a social animal—though not as a political animal—and recognizing the necessity for communication. Nothing can more vividly illustrate this change than our present attitude toward solitary confinement, as contrasted with the attitude of a hundred and fifty years ago. At that time solitary confinement was not thought of as a punishment, but a speedy and effective type of reform therapy: the individual was confronted with himself and learned what his mistakes had been. He was safe from the contamination of society. Now it is considered the harshest punishment that can be inflicted.

[From a lecture at the University of Massachusetts, Autumn 1966]

The process of self-definition cannot go on by itself; it calls for the presence of others, and people of the younger generation know this better than anyone else. It is a dialog, not a monolog, and that is why existential writers in particular attach such importance to language, to communication. Existence means *shared* existence. We are all increasingly dependent on the presence of our fellow men—not necessarily on their approval; their reaction to our existence is just as essential.

The results of this tendency to get together, informally and perhaps briefly, are very evident. Urbanization is one obvious example; but it is visible on a much smaller scale as well. What we are likely to notice, when we look at the social life of the average American small town or city, is that the favorite places of social interaction are not the institutions which previous generations preferred: the church, the public building, the public square, the club or lodge, or the so-called community center or the school. These are no longer popular except on special occasions. We have found other places for meeting together.

A Swiss sociologist* has observed that much contemporary planning theory is actually based on only those needs which we share with animals—shelter, food, recreation, movement, work, or defense. This would certainly be a logical inheritance from the nineteenth century, because it ignores what we now consider our most essentially human trait—our need to communicate, to be social. In any case, without the assistance or guidance of planners we are beginning to establish places for informal social interaction; and these places are well worth study.

---

* See Paul Hotz, "Planning of Mice and Men," *Landscape*, 16:2, pp. 12–14.

If the desire for communication is one of the most important aspects of our drive for self-definition, then the highway is the prime symbol of this drive. Communication can be defined in several ways: it means passage from one place to another, and it means the transmitting of a message. In terms of the highway, it means an unending flow of traffic—perhaps much of it essentially aimless, a kind of search for some place or person to help reinforce our identity; it also means the signs and billboards and lights and signals—a chorus of communications such as no generation has ever before seen. We are told that this confused collection of messages is undermining our sanity, but we somehow contrive to find our way through it. We may not enjoy it, but one virtue of our being communications-minded is that we have learned how to filter out those communications which don't concern us. We deal with the familiar, recognizable symbols.

It is along the highway, particularly in the built-up areas, that we can best see that kind of exhibitionist, self-identifying architecture which is designed to convey as loudly and as vividly as possible some assertion of identity to the passerby —motels, drive-in establishments, shopping centers, even factories and office buildings and churches.

None of these signs and structures possesses an *essential* identity: they seek to establish a kind of existential identity by setting up a brief dialog: "See me!" they cry; and we answer, "I see you; you're a root beer stand (or a drive-in movie)." They are like those teen-agers, more numerous in the West, who wear their identity carved on their belts or on the backs of their jackets.

The highway has many shortcomings, aesthetic, economic, and social; it is often ugly, inefficient, and destructive to many communities. Yet even the most cluttered, the most garish and vulgar specimen has an immense potential. Moreover, the highway strip is developing a remarkable aesthetic style of its own. Its lighting effects—not merely the neon signs but the indirect lighting of filling stations and drive-ins —are often extremely handsome; so are the bright clear colors of the buildings and installations; so are the open spaces, even though they are not coordinated. It often seems that America is evolving a taste for a new kind of beauty: clean-cut geometric forms, primary colors, vast smooth surfaces and wide spaces uninterrupted by any detail, and bright lights. It is the beauty of newness, efficiency, and cleanliness, but to date, at least, it represents a thoroughly unsophisticated popular taste.

What is more significant is the social appeal of the highway strip, the chosen area of brief informal communication and social interaction. Drive through any medium-sized community in America after dark and you will at once see all the vitality is concentrated here—not along Main Street, and certainly not in the residential areas. This is where you will find the mixed public we so long to have in our central business district: teenagers, transients, people in search of amusement, doing business, alone and in group. And this is no ordinary street scene; this is specifically American.

The art and architecture of the strip is designed to attract. For all its flashiness it respects something like the human scale, it seeks to communicate, and does so very successfully. Its topical frame of reference—the use of popular names, symbols, effects—even its very flimsiness and temporary quality make it congenial for informal temporary social intercourse, for it is a jumbled reminder of all current enthusiasms—atomic energy, space travel, Acapulco, folksinging, computers, Danish contemporary, health foods, hot-rod racing, and so on. And part of this congenial atmosphere is that it prescribes no traditional behavior; unlike the conventional park or even the public square, the strip allows almost complete freedom of conduct and dress.

The chief reason for the popularity of the strip, however, is that it is entirely adjusted to the automobile; it does not try to separate the automobile from its driver. It is characteristic of this generation to use not only the environment to create its identity but to use objects as well; and one of the most useful objects from this point of view is the automobile. It is adaptable, mobile, a means to gregariousness, and is common enough to be a recognizable means of communication in both senses of the word.

The adversary of the automobile is not the pedestrian as we may sometimes think, but the plot of land. Until about sixty years ago we believed in this country that possession of land and work on it created our identity. Everyone was supposed to have a homestead in order to be a good citizen and a well-rounded individual. To express the idea existentially, land was the object men could best use in their search for identity. The belief, of course, is very ancient and it is still held by many people. But it is doubtful if ever again in America will it have the same almost religious appeal. What has happened is that the land changed its status; it became a commodity, something which could be translated into money. We looked around for another usable object—and behold! the automobile appeared.

When we speak of the auto as a status symbol (as was fashionable a few years ago), we are speaking of new cars only; the average used car or jalopy is no status symbol of any sort. It is nevertheless an intimate part of its owner's identity. We all know the infinite variety of purposes the automobile serves—some very utilitarian some social, and many of them psychological. The way we drive it, the way we work on it, the way we decorate it, all serve to identify us. A plausible theory could be developed that the greater the number of emotional problems there are among the young men in a family, the more cars you see in the front yard; working on a car is one of those tell-tale signs of emotional disturbances like a housewife's moving the furniture around; in both cases manipulating the environment serves as an outlet. Whatever the psychological role of the automobile, we do not like being separated from it for very long, particularly when we are not sure of ourselves. And the strip is a tacit recognition of this relationship.

There are good reasons for insisting on a separation between cars and people in certain parts of town, for the failure to separate them has caused the ruin of many places. We will not solve this problem, however, until we learn to see the car in another more personal light; we have thought of it too much in terms of transportation. In Holland they have recognized the importance of the car in their new recreation areas; sociologists there have defined recreational needs in what can be called existential terms: "the need for sociability, the need to use one's own personal possessions [automobile], the need to collect experiences, and the need to run dangers."

The highway is merely one, though the most important, of these new centers of sociability. The others are the recreation area, the campground, and the motorsport track. All of these have at least one trait in common: the importance of the automobile. Should we not develop more of these meeting places, and improve the ones which already exist? This is something the environmental designer can learn to do. Pedestrian malls and recreation and shopping areas which exclude the car are very desirable and can be made true works of art; but an even greater challenge is designing to integrate the automobile into certain types of gathering places. And the best place to study this sort of problem is along the highway strip.

Is this sort of intercourse the ultimate in human society? A landscape catering to our gregarious instincts is certainly better than one which isolates us; but are we not capable of something more productive and permanent? We are learning to redefine man as a social animal but we are not yet learning to define him as a political animal. We are evolving a social landscape as well, but this is not the ultimate in environmental design. A landscape allowed to expand to suit temporary needs leaves a great deal to be desired. Each of us feels the need for something permanent in the world surrounding us, just as we feel the need for a permanent identity for ourselves. This is not merely a matter of security or of objection to change. It is a matter of satisfying a fundamental human urge to be a part of an order which is more lasting than we are: a moral or ethical order which transcends our individual existence. The Romantic generations derived this kind of satisfaction from their feeling of oneness with nature. What do we have to take its place?

It is possible for the landscape to provide us with some symbols of permanent values. It is possible for it to provide us with landmarks to reassure us that we are not rootless individuals without identity or place, but are part of a larger scheme. The landscape can do much to reinforce our identity as political beings.

The Public Landscape

THE PUBLIC OR POLITICAL landscape is quite distinct from the natural landscape or the economic landscape or the private landscape, though no more important than these. The architectural concept of the megastructure, popular several years ago, was roughly that of a skeletal framework comprising the essential functions of the building, into which are inserted the individual, more or less temporary, installations. The advantages of the megastructure are that the individual is provided with certain necessary facilities and also a greater freedom of choice. The megastructure is *prior* to the individual installation and, presumably, more lasting.

Few of us realize that there is another kind of megastructure, a megastructure in terms of a whole environment; one of the oldest creations of man. This megastructure consisting of the environment organized by man can be called the public landscape. A more correct term would be the political landscape; but since we associate that word not with citizenship as we should, but with politicians and politics, the term public is more effective.

There are certain installations, modifications of the physical environment that every organized community has to have if it is to function and endure. Among these are boundaries, roads, public places, and monuments. In some societies their primary purpose is to help keep the state physically intact. In others their purpose is also to insure a certain quality in the lives of the citizens—to promote civilization.

This public landscape is invariably the result of an historical process. We can say of it what we have said of the

[From a lecture at the University of Massachusetts, Autumn 1966]

architectural megastructure: it is *prior* to the individual citizen or individual holding. The public landscape is prior to the private landscape. But unlike its architectural counterpart, the public landscape can and does change, and that is why it is of interest to us now: we must change the existing public landscape if we are once more to have a political identity.

It is futile to ask which of these features of the public landscape comes first. The boundary is in many ways the most interesting because it arouses the most emotion and produces the most action and reaction; not in reference to international wars inspired by boundary disputes but to our own individual response to the concept of the boundary or limit. Nothing was more typical of the nineteenth century than chronic discontent with boundaries; they were almost always looked upon either as obstacles to legitimate expansion or as obstacles to friendship and free communication. Many years ago Robert Frost gave a reading of his poem "Mending Wall."* In it there is a line which goes: "Good fences make good neighbors." When Frost had finished, a lady spoke up indignantly from the back of the room: "But Mr. Frost, don't you believe in the League of Nations?" For a world without boundaries was part of the old-fashioned liberal dream. Does the present generation share this conviction, or are boundaries perhaps coming back into favor —if not in international affairs at least in everyday life? It is well to remember that the word means *that which binds together*; a boundary is what makes it possible for a society to have its own individuality. And this is true of the individual holding also. Before the Enclosure Act in sixteenth-century

Complete Works of Robert Frost (New York: Holt, Rinehart, and Winston, 1949), p. 47.

England, when all the village livestock ran together and all crops were cultivated in common, it was impossible to raise high-grade produce or cattle. It was only after the enclosures that England became famous for its sheep and its beef. Do we not sometimes pay our respects to the idea of a landscape without boundaries in the restrictive sense, but in practice want them? We want zoning, national parks, electoral districts that are just; we want privacy. If any difference can be discerned, it is that the boundaries in the past were intended to insure self-sufficiency whereas now we think of interdependence. It is a subject every environmental planner should explore: what should be included within a boundary and how are we to locate them? for the boundary is an essential element in the public landscape. Reinhold Niebuhr says: "The fence and the boundary line are the symbols of the spirit of justice. They set the limits upon each man's interest to prevent one from taking advantage of the other." *

The second element in the public landscape that needs redefinition is the public road or highway. The highway is playing an increasingly vital role in our modern landscape and has become the most familiar symbol of informal gregariousness. This has not been its role in the past, nor will it necessarily be its role in the future. The highway stands for unity. It is that installation which joins one part of the public landscape to another, which enables organized society to make its influence felt everywhere. The highway is in essence a right of way, something which only a sovereign state can establish and which it establishes for its own purposes. Maintenance and construction are therefore quite

The Nature and Destiny of Man, Vol. ii, *Human Destiny* (New York: Charles Scribner's Sons, 1943), p. 252.

separate aspects. The classical King's Highway existed to
permit the king to move troops and officials as rapidly as
possible from one part of the country to another. American
custom took over this social interpretation of the highway
or the public road. In the villages of Colonial New England
the establishing of roads was the prerogative of the town
officials, for it was thought essential that there be roads from
every farm to the church or meetinghouse if the landowners
were to serve in their capacity as voters. In the same manner,
in the early years of the Republic, public roads were almost
always thought of and built as instruments for achieving
social unity—for the speedy distribution of mail, and for the
movement of troops, and for making distant settlements
accessible to the central government. They were not intended
primarily for commerce or economic development, although
they also served those ends.

The distinction between the road as a means of achieving
unity and the road as a means for encouraging economic
activity may seem to be hairsplitting; but it is a distinction
of some importance. The road as an economic (or tourist)
facility is thought of in terms of its economic returns; it is
accordingly designed and located with a particular traffic in
mind, and it is to the interest of its builders to encourage
that kind of traffic. In a sense it is a public utility, operated
by the state for the benefit of its chief users, like the gas and
telephone companies. There is nothing wrong in this kind
of road, and we are building more and more of them. But the
public road as a social installation has quite a different character. It is built because it will encourage unity, because it will
bring citizens together. Even if a road to the meetinghouse
were used only twice a week it was thought to be justified. In
this sense the road is a social institution, like a law court or a

fire station: something which every citizen has to have, even though he may not use it often and even though he cannot afford the costs all by himself. In the West you see long country roads with perhaps four or five families on them; but they are maintained as well as possible not only because they are used by the rural free delivery and the school bus, but because these few families are entitled to be part of the community. Tradition keeps this other interpretation of the public road alive in small communities, but we need to reinvigorate it. We need to think of some roads and streets purely and simply in terms of their contribution to unity, and this means roads which lead to some social destination. The winding roads of our more prosperous suburbs, typically enough, lead merely to individual destinations, and the roads of a grid system lead nowhere at all: they are centrifugal in nature.

Another feature of the public landscape is the public meeting place. It is hardly necessary to underscore the importance of this installation to the present generation of environmental planners. We must bear in mind that the public space, whether in the city or the village, can assume many different forms, some of them a great deal more productive than others. It can be an area exclusively reserved for the coming together of citizens. Aristotle, for instance, specifies a square where nothing would be bought or sold, and no members of the lower orders or countrymen were allowed unless summoned by the authorities. On the other hand in many communities the public square is the market place. The nineteeth century transformed many places of public assembly into parks; elsewhere they have been pre-empted by public buildings and parking lots, or playgrounds for children. All of these are necessary functions, but they are not functions appropriate to a gathering place which is, in terms of the public landscape, an area where we are particularly aware of our identity as citizens. The federal government has been guilty of ignoring this political function. Either for fear of being pompous, or from indifference, it is everywhere destroying public gathering places near or around federal buildings. Small-town post offices, formerly congenial gathering places, have been landscaped and isolated; and the very term "public building" has become a contradiction: no one in his right mind now goes into a public building except on business. Only the county courthouse still remains true to its own function. The question is, of course, what form the public gathering place should assume. The Communist countries seem to be devising their own versions. One thing can be said: there must be many more such places, large and small, scattered throughout our communities.

There is one final feature of the public landscape: the monument. We usually think of the monument as a permanent construction designed to keep alive the memory of a person or an event, and we give it a public character and a public location. Its form varies from one period to another: we no longer build triumphal arches or even erect statues of individuals; we are more and more inclined to consider a whole environment a monument—a park, a grove of trees, an auditorium. But regardless of its form, the monument continues to serve more or less the same function: it is a reminder of the past, it is a symbol of another community to which we belong: the community of those who have died. If the public square is a reminder of the present, the monument is a reminder of promises made, or origins which we are inclined to forget. This is not the place to discuss the changes in the kind of monuments we choose. But here is an example: in the early nineteenth century our graveyards were collections of tombstones—monuments in the old-fashioned use of the word—a community of individual graves, and it was the individual dead whom we commemorated. But by the middle of the century the cemetery had become a beautifully landscaped park, through which one wandered. It was as if the whole area had become a monument, and as if the individual dead had become part of the community of nature with its own kind of resurrection. It would appear that a very strong element in our enthusiasm for natural parks (as distinguished from city parks) is this sentiment for the cemetery as a monument—a place of communion with invisible spirits. It may well be stretching the use of the word "monument" to include national parks and wilderness areas—though the Department of the Interior designates some nine million acres as national monuments. Nevertheless there is an underlying similiarity of function between the triumphal arch, the tombstone, and the national park.

Each culture has its own concept of that invisible community to which it owes loyalty and from which it draws inspiration; but all these are reminders of ancient obligations, all of them are publicly honored, all of them are identified with holidays and public commemoration. The designing and locating of appropriate monuments in the new public landscape will likely be one of the most difficult jobs of the coming generation of environmental designers; because this is not simply a matter of recreation, it is a matter of reminding, of making people think.

We have touched on merely four features of the public landscape: boundary, highway, meeting place, and monument. The intelligent design of these features would do much to enrich our public existence. They can make it easier for

us to identify ourselves as active members of the political
community and give some permanent and creative form to
our gregariousness. The environmental megastructure—to
revert to the earlier comparison—supplies essential facilities
for a civilized way of life; it thereby fosters the private landscape, the private realm. A properly functioning public landscape allows the private landscape to specialize and achieve
individuality.

This is not to say that all we need do is reform the public
landscape; the economic landscape and the natural landscape
clamor for attention. But the study of the political aspects of
the landscape should have priority. For this is how environmental design can take its place among the humanities: not
by the diligent use of computers, nor by the concentrating
on aesthetics. The primary task is to design environments
where it will be possible for men to lead the lives of free
and responsible citizens, where they can give expression to
the social or political side of their nature.

Would a landscape or a city conceived of in these terms
be beautiful? Not necessarily; but it would remind us of
order and unity and justice, and it is quite possible that in
time we would learn to find beauty in these characteristics.
The permanent aspects of our environment are those which
matter most. If we produce a handsome and serviceable megastructure we can tolerate the shortcomings of the individual
environment, which in any case lasts only a few years.